Macroeconomic Policy
and the Future of Capitalism

In Memory of Marie Heřmanská, née Glocová

Macroeconomic Policy and the Future of Capitalism

The Revenge of the Rentiers and the Threat to Prosperity

John Smithin

York University, Canada

Edward Elgar
Cheltenham, UK • Brookfield, US

Published by
Edward Elgar Publishing Limited
8 Lansdown Place
Cheltenham
Glos GL50 2HU
UK

Edward Elgar Publishing Company
Old Post Road
Brookfield
Vermont 05036
US

British Library Cataloguing in Publication Data
Smithin, John N.
 Macroeconomic policy and the future of capitalism : the
 revenge of the rentiers and the threat to prosperity
 1. Macroeconomics   2. Capitalism   3. Economic policy
 I. Title
 339.5

Library of Congress Cataloguing in Publication Data
Smithin, John.
 Macroeconomic policy and the future of capitalism: the revenge of
 the rentiers and the threat to prosperity / John Smithin.
  Includes bibliographical references and index.
  1. Monetary policy—History—20th century.   2. Keynesian
 economics—History—20th century.   3. Capitalism—History—20th
 century.   4. Macroeconomics—History—20th century.
 5. International finance—History—20th century.   6. Economic
 history—20th century.   I. Title.
 HG230.3.S64   1996
 339.5'3'09049—dc20   95–51454
                                                             CIP

ISBN 1 85278 731 7 (cased)
    1 85278 745 7 (paperback)

Printed and bound in Great Britain by Biddles Limited, Guildford and King's Lynn

Contents

Preface

This book brings together, I hope in a coherent and persuasive manner, some ideas on contemporary macroeconomic policy issues which I first explored in my *Macroeconomics After Thatcher and Reagan* (1990), and on some key issues in theoretical monetary economics discussed in my *Controversies in Monetary Economics* (1994a). In the forewords to those volumes I acknowledged the help of several colleagues in preparing them for publication, on both specific and general matters. I would like those acknowledgements to stand, at one remove, for the current work also.

The subtitle 'The Revenge of the Rentiers' is obviously a reference to chapter 24 of Keynes's *The General Theory* (1936, 376) in which he suggested that adoption of the policy principles he was advocating would lead to the 'euthanasia of the rentier'. The financial reaction in the last quarter of the twentieth century, which has led to the wholesale rejection of anything resembling 'the social philosophy towards which the General Theory might lead' (1936, 372), clearly does lend itself to an image of 'scores being settled' on the part of financial capital. What I suggest is that a new compromise must be achieved if the underlying prosperity of the economic system is to be maintained. I first used the expression in a talk to the Economic Literacy Workshop organized by TLCSAC/LWAG in Toronto in February 1995. I am grateful to Kim Jarvi for extending the invitation and making the arrangements on that occasion. I also gave a talk with the same title at the University of Hohenheim, Germany, at the invitation of Harald Hagemann, in October 1995.

John Grieve-Smith, Geoff Harcourt and Vishnu Padayachee all read the complete manuscript during my visit to Robinson College, Cambridge, in the Michaelmas (Fall) term 1995, and I am grateful for their comments and reactions.

I would like to thank Edward Elgar and his staff, in particular Julie Leppard and Dymphna Evans, for their support and encouragement for this project. It was Dymphna Evans who finally suggested the main title, which describes the contents far more accurately than any of the alternatives I had been able to come up with.

Hana Smithin, as always, has been my main guiding light and inspiration. She has pored over every chapter in detail, and insisted that the ideas be expressed clearly, and with a minimum of the usual academic jargon. If I have succeeded in this, it is because of her.

1. Prosperity and austerity

INTRODUCTION

The so-called babyboom generation, born in the years immediately after World War II in the industrialized or developed nations, grew up with a perspective on economic affairs which is probably unique in human history. In contrast to the youth of other times and other places, they found themselves in a world in which economic prosperity and, even more importantly, economic security, were more-or-less taken for granted.

'You've never had it so good', the British Prime Minister, Harold Macmillan, is reputed to have told his electorate in 1959. In fact, even if his grammar left something to be desired, the sentiment was not inaccurate. For the traditional ruling class in Britain, it is true, the period was viewed as one of national decline. They had lost an Empire, and Britain's economic position *relative* to that of other nations was certainly declining. Yet, for the average citizen the standard of living in absolute terms was greater than at any time in the nation's history and the prospects of income and employment *security* were incomparably better.

If this was true in Britain, in relative decline, then obviously it was so *a fortiori* in the other industrialized nations in North America, Europe, and, soon after, Japan, all of whom were outstripping the 'first industrial nation' in the economic growth leagues. Middle-class college students in the USA in the 1960s, for example, notoriously felt that they could always afford to drop out of school to explore alternative lifestyles, travel, etc., at least for a year or two, without damage to their ultimate career prospects and living standards.

Such luxuries had obviously been denied to the previous generation. The capitalist economic system had all but collapsed in the Great Depression of the 1930s. This had made the totalitarian reaction to capitalism, whether in the form of National Socialism, Fascism, or Communism, seem plausible and even desirable to many, and in turn led to a level of barbarism and human suffering which had threatened the survival of the civilization.

Unfortunately also, the generations coming *after* the babyboomers were not able to enjoy such apparently desirable prospects, and the boomers themselves, in mid-career, have seen the rules change on them in the middle of the game. There has been no economic collapse of the magnitude of the 1930s, but, economic security, in particular, has effectively disappeared for large numbers of people. The ancient cycle of boom and bust, which had been thought to have been eliminated in the first 25 years or so after World War II, has returned with a vengeance. There was an old notion in Marxism that the existence of a 'reserve army of the unemployed' is an absolute necessity for the efficient functioning of capitalism. It is a devastating indictment of the new era that this concept has been revived, enthusiastically welcomed, and actually put into practice by orthodox policymakers in the modern world, albeit under different names, such as the NAIRU[1] or the 'natural rate' of unemployment. There is little attempt to disguise the new attitude in official reports and commentary. McQuaig (1995: 151–2), for example, quotes from a Bank of Canada technical paper which describes how 'unemployment acts as a signal to individuals to change their expectations about future salary and wage increases', and from a Bank for International Settlements (BIS) report advocating the need for 'restrictive demand management' on a worldwide scale in order to achieve 'more satisfactory levels of *un*employment' (emphasis added). The idea is simply that a certain level of unemployment is necessary to discipline the workforce and persuade them to accept less.

The obvious questions to ask are how this state of affairs has been allowed to develop and what, if anything, can be done about it? People living in the industrialized world of the early 1960s must have congratulated themselves on the distance they had travelled between the 'buddy can you spare a dime' of the 1930s and 'you've never had it so good' in their own time. But the gulf between the optimism of the 1960s and our own economically nervous and insecure era is almost as wide, even if a disaster of the magnitude of the 1930s has not yet occurred.

WHAT WENT WRONG?

The economics profession, in the sense of economic researchers employed in academia and 'thinktanks' (most of whom enjoy perfect job security themselves), has obviously played a role in the change of climate. Its members have apparently been only too willing to devise complex mathematical theories whose bottom line is to justify, on an ostensibly scientific basis, policies whereby others lose their jobs or businesses.[2] More likely, however, the change in academic economic theory, profound though it has been, is a reflection of other deeper forces in society militating for change. Academics, after all, respond to market incentives just like anybody else, and if there is a demand for theories which explain or defend a particular point of view, there will likely be an adequate supply.

The conventional explanation of what has occurred in recent years would portray the postwar policymakers as having been entirely in the grip of flawed 'Keynesian' theories, which then spectacularly failed in the 1970s, and were actually responsible for the economic ills of that decade. The change in economic theory since that time is then supposedly a return to traditional wisdom, or hard-headed common sense, and the unpalatable policy measures which have been taken in the 1980s and 1990s are simply the bad medicine which, unpleasant though it seems, is necessary to eventually restore the patient to health. What this view does not explain, however, is why the system came so near to collapse in the 1930s when the traditional views were also in the ascendant, and why alternative remedies, now bitterly denounced as witchcraft, did apparently succeed, to an unprecedented degree, for at least a quarter of a century?

It is suggested here that there is an alternative explanation of the course of macroeconomic events since World War II. This is that the good years were actually the result of a historically unique compromise between the competing economic interest groups in the capitalist economy, which worked out, as sensible comprises often do, to the benefit of all concerned. This compromise was certainly influenced to some extent by Keynesian theory. However, this factor should not be exaggerated as it is also obvious in retrospect that the Keynesian theory was far from correctly understood either by the academics or policymakers of the time. The other factor making for compromise was more plausibly the awfulness of the alternatives, either economic breakdown or totalitarianism, which meant that something had to be done to save the system. Subsequent events can then be explained by the *breakdown* of the compromise in the key decade of the 1970s, and the reaction or backlash to this from one of the main interest groups concerned, the consequences of which we are living with to this day.

MONEY: THE ROOT OF ALL EVIL?

The essence of the capitalist economy is that it is a monetary economy, what Keynes long ago called a 'monetary production economy' (Smithin, 1994a). This continues to be the case even if the concept of money itself is constantly undergoing metamorphosis as technology and social institutions change. Production and employment decisions are made by those who must hire the factors of production by making monetary payments, and whose receipts from the eventual sale of output are also in terms of money. Output and employment outcomes depend upon expectations of money receipts relative to money costs. The ultimate reward structure of the society, and the distribution of power and prestige, also depends upon the accumulation of wealth denominated in monetary or financial terms. This immediately creates a potential conflict between those engaged in the production and distribution of goods and services, including both business, in the sense of entrepreneurs and industrial corporations, and labour; and those who have already accumulated substantial financial wealth, whether these are individual 'rentiers' or, more realistically in the present day, financial corporations and institutions.[3] Life is made easier for the former by 'cheap money' and rising prices, as the value of goods-in-process appreciates on their hands, stimulating both output and employment, whereas the same circumstances threaten the entrenched position of the latter group.

In the 1930s, the opposite situation was in place. Prices were actually falling, and even if nominal interest rates were very low, *real* interest rates, that is the difference between interest rates quoted in the marketplace and the expected inflation rate, were very high (Temin, 1989). This would be fine for anybody already possessing a large fortune (and who had not lost it in the stock market crash). One's dollars or pounds or yen could buy more every day. However, it would be an impossible situation for anyone who planned to borrow money to build a factory or buy a farm. The real burden of the original debt would similarly be increasing every day, and the price of the final product would be falling. It would be an impossible situation also for anyone who relied on finding employment on those farms or in the factories. Obviously, as in the 1930s, this logic can be pushed too far, even from the point of view of those who seemingly benefit. If the system eventually collapses altogether, and there is nothing to buy, even the money fortunes will be worthless.

The opposite case would be one in which there was a very high rate of inflation and real interest rates were negative, meaning that the nominal rate of interest on financial instruments is *not* enough to compensate wealthholders for inflation. Superficially, this is now an excellent situation in which to conduct business. The prices of final goods are continually rising and the financiers are effectively *paying* the entrepreneurs for holding inventory and making capital investments. But, obviously, this is also not a viable or stable situation. The ultimate incentive structure of the society is breaking down, because presumably the entrepreneurs (and workers) would also eventually like to make some money which then retains its value. If they will themselves inevitably be expropriated as others are being expropriated today, it will come to seem that there is little point in entering into productive activity in the first place.

THE 'REVENGE OF THE RENTIERS'

From this perspective, the reasonably prosperous years for the first quarter century after World War II can be seen as a workable compromise between the competing economic interest groups. The pressure of aggregate demand was maintained by the use of policies influenced by Keynesian ideas, and real interest rates were kept reasonably low by the monetary authorities, at this time, principally, the US Federal Reserve System. This provided the space in which both 'big business' and 'big labour' could grow and prosper. From the point of view of the rentier or financial interests, however, even if real interest rates were kept relatively low, they were at least positive, and the value of financial capital could still be maintained. Higher rates of return would surely have been welcome, but, in the circumstances, to take what was offered no doubt seemed a reasonable course of action when compared to the potential collapse of the entire system in the immediately preceding generation.

The real point about the 1970s, however, was that this compromise was rudely shattered. Monetary authorities around the world responded to the various economic difficulties of the decade, such as the aftermath of the Vietnam War and the 'oil shocks' with still more aggressively inflationary and cheap money policies. The nightmare, from the rentier point of view, of negative real rates of interest, actually became a reality in many jurisdictions. As suggested, although this may seem like a good idea from the point of view of borrowers, such as residential homeowners, it is doubtful that capitalism is viable as a social system on these terms. The result was ultimately a political revolution around the years 1979 to 1982, the most important feature of which was the 'capture' of central banks by rentier interests, and their conversion thereafter to exclusively 'hard money', high interest, and anti-inflation policies. This was the 'Revenge of the Rentiers' after the depredations of the 1970s. Since that time the rhetoric of the macroeconomic policy debate has focused almost entirely on financial issues, such as the need to cure inflation, the need to balance the government budget, the need to maintain the value of the exchange rate, and so on. In a very real sense, however, the ultimate purpose behind the 'conservative' prescriptions on all of these issues is to maintain and increase the real rate of return to financial capital.

Our policymakers have, in fact, been highly successful in this objective for the most part. As indicated earlier, however, there is a very real danger that this reaction has gone too far, and that the prosperity of the real economy, on which everybody's well-being ultimately depends, is in danger. The profitability of industry, the growth of real wages, and the security of employment have essentially been sacrificed in the over-enthusiastic attempt to right the wrongs of the 1970s. To many people, the capitalistic economic system no doubt seems doubly secure today due to the demise of one of the main alternatives on offer, communism, in the years after 1989. There is reason to doubt, however, that it will continue to be so if the system itself continues to fail to deliver a secure prosperity in the way that it once seemed capable of doing. It is worth reflecting that one of the myriad causes of the collapse of communism, after all, was the effective drying up of handouts from, and markets in, the West, due to the West's own economic difficulties.

The remedy for all of these ills, however, seems fairly obvious. What seems to be required is simply a return to the earlier compromise of the 1950s and 1960s. Real interest rates should be kept lower than they have typically been in the 1980s and 1990s, but should not be allowed to fall negative as in the 1970s, and the pressure of aggregate demand should be maintained. The real problems, however, have been obscured by the symbolic and totemic nature of the debate, with the focus on such issues as inflation, budget deficits, and the prestige to be conferred by a strong currency, rather than the real question of what constitutes a reasonable reward for various types of effort in the social system of the day.

The real issues are studiously avoided by contemporary economic theorists, for whom any discussion in these terms is apparently anathema. Significantly, the main theoretical device employed by contemporary macroeconomists is that of the 'representative agent' who is buyer and seller, worker and employer, salesperson, consumer, accountant, and banker, all in one. The problems of the economy as a whole are treated as if they are identical with the problems of a single person, whose opinions supposedly reflect those of society as a whole. It is fairly easy to provide a mathematical representation of this individual's 'optimization problem', provided that his or her tastes and preferences and the relevant constraints are properly specified. With only one economic actor, however, it is somewhat more difficult, to say the least, for the contemporary academic economist to identity the potential sources of social tension and suggest a remedy.

PLAN OF THE BOOK

In what follows, chapter 2, 'The Main Macroeconomic Trends of the Twentieth Century', provides a brief and selective survey of macroeconomic history, in order to provide some factual background for the interpretative chapters which follow. It actually goes back even further than the twentieth century, as there is also a discussion of the gold standard era of *c.* 1870 to 1914.

Chapter 3 then goes on to deal with the interface between 'Politics and Economics', which is particularly necessary in the case of this volume. Some of the ideas presented will no doubt seem 'left-wing' to certain politically committed readers, while other ideas (and possibly even the same ideas) will seem 'right-wing' to different individuals. In fact, they are neither. In chapter 4, 'The Power of Ideas', the impact of purely intellectual developments in economic theory is then discussed and criticized.

There follow three chapters, chapter 5, 'Inflation and the Economy', chapter 6, 'Cause and Effect in the Relationship between Budget Deficits and the Rate of Interest', and chapter 7, 'What Should be Done about the Balance of Payments and the Exchange Rate?', which deal separately with each of the three main issues which dominate the contemporary macroeconomic debate. The main thesis of the book is set out in chapter 5, dealing with the obsession with inflation which is so characteristic of current economic thinking, while chapters 6 and 7 deal with the consequences of this obsession for the public finances and international economic relations, respectively.

Chapter 8, 'Macroeconomics and the Stock Market', deals with the relationship between the macroeconomic events discussed in earlier chapters and the behaviour of the stock market. It is argued that the erratic ups and downs of the latter actually provide considerable evidence in favour of the interpretation of events put forward in this book.

Finally, chapter 9 offers some brief concluding remarks.

NOTES

1. The 'non-accelerating inflation rate of unemployment'.
2. Keynes had hoped that one day economists would be as useful to society as dentists. But how useful would dentists actually be if they advised their patients not to bother with dental hygiene on the grounds of a 'policy ineffectiveness' theorem for dental policy? Or, if their only suggested remedy for a minor cavity was extraction with no anaesthetic?
3. The term 'rentiers' obviously derives from the French, and historically referred to agricultural landlords. More recent usage tends to have a financial connotation, meaning persons whose main income consists of interest on financial investments. Keynes (1923; 1971), for example, uses the term in this sense. The *Oxford English Dictionary* defines 'rentier' as: 'a person living on dividends from property, investments, etc.'

2. The main macroeconomic trends of the twentieth century

INTRODUCTION

The purpose of this chapter is to illustrate the main trends, key events, and turning points in the macroeconomic history of the past 100 years or so. The objective is to provide at least a sketch of the factual background, to illustrate the context of the interpretative chapters which follow. The focus is mainly on the experience of what might (loosely) be called the industrialized or 'developed' nations, say today's G7. The key players in the world economy for much of the period under discussion were obviously, first, Britain, and then the USA. Later, their erstwhile antagonists of World War II, Germany and Japan, became important. The problems of development and underdevelopment are not explicitly treated, but an approach to these issues is at least implicit in the general discussion. The events and trends to be considered are those which seem to be the most relevant from the point of view of the overall approach of the book.

THE WORLD OF THE GOLD STANDARD

The Nobel prize-winning economist, Sir John Hicks (1986), once made a very striking comparison between the world economy into which he was born (in 1904) and that of the late twentieth century, which he lived to see. His main point was the far greater stability of money *prices* in the earlier period rather than the later, and even more important, the confident expectation that they would stay that way.

It is interesting that Hicks did not mention the apparently obvious things which would likely occur to the contemporary business executive, such as computers, information technology, robotics and so on. On reflection, though, this is surely correct, because, paradoxically, rapid technical change has actually been the one 'permanent' feature of the world economy since the Industrial Revolution. It was just as much a strategic issue for individuals and firms at the beginning of the twentieth century as at its end. The upheavals caused by automobiles, the dawn of air travel, electrification, telephones, etc., were clearly both as disruptive and/or beneficial to people living at the time as the 'information super-highway' threatens to be today.

Nor did Hicks mention the type of issues later summed up by the popular expression, 'globalization', again for good reasons. In fact, to all intents and purposes a 'global, internationally competitive' economy was already in existence a hundred years ago, albeit a lower level of technology. As Keynes (1920: 11–13) had put in describing the pre-World War I world:

> The inhabitant of London could order by telephone, sipping his morning tea in bed, the various products of the whole earth, in such quantity as he might see fit, and reasonably expect their early delivery upon his doorstep; he could...by the same means adventure his wealth in the natural resources and new enterprises of any quarter of the world...He could secure forthwith...cheap and comfortable means of transit to any country or climate without passport or other formality... and...proceed abroad to foreign quarters...bearing coined wealth upon his person, and would consider himself greatly aggrieved and much surprised at the least interference...he regarded this state of affairs as normal, certain, and permanent ...The projects of militarism and imperialism...which were to play serpent to this paradise...appeared to exercise almost no influence at all on the ordinary course of economic and social life, *the internationalization of which was nearly complete in practice.* (emphasis added)

It was this world which was destroyed by the collapse of civilization in the 1914–18 war, and which liberal economists spent the rest of the twentieth century trying to build up again.

The expectation of stable prices before World War I, however, does decisively differentiate the period from anything that was to follow. This was an era, after all, in which the price of drinks in a bar, or the price of a haircut in a barbershop, might actually be cut into a glass mirror or window. Hicks (1986: 20) points out that when he was born the price of postage stamps, and even of rail fares, had not changed, or hardly changed, for a half-century. Here is one of the great psychological differences between the world economy of 100 years ago and that of more recent times. Throughout the second half of the twentieth century, inflation, at different rates in different jurisdictions, has simply been a fact of life and stable prices certainly could not be taken for granted. Even by the mid-1990s, after a period in which rigorous 'zero-inflation' policies had been pursued with some success in several jurisdictions, average consumer price inflation in the G7 was still positive (forecast at around 2.5 per cent for 1995),[1] and there is certainly no 50-year track record of anything like price stability to influence future expectations.

The reasonably confident expectation of price stability in the pre-World War I period, was, presumably, primarily due to the strict adherence of most of the major trading nations to the monetary regime of the international gold standard. Each of the main currencies was convertible into gold at a fixed rate. This would imply what is now known as a 'fixed exchange rate regime'. If the US dollar is defined as being equal to a certain quantity of gold, as is the pound sterling, the French franc, the German mark, etc., this will fix the relative values of the currencies themselves within very narrow limits.[2] Thus, the British pound was equal to 4.86 dollars, 25 francs, 20 marks, (roughly) 10 Japanese yen, and so on (Hicks, 1986). As long as the gold standard could be maintained, therefore, it was certainly the case that *external* price stability would be assured.

The gold standard as a genuinely international phenomenon was actually of fairly recent provenance at the turn of the twentieth century. Its effective starting point is usually dated from around 1873, when the USA passed legislation to 'de-monetize' silver,[3] and hence became a full member of the gold standard community. Nonetheless, there was a long history of gold-based monetary systems in other nations, and by the end of the nineteenth century the gold standard seems to have been believed to be a more or less permanent fixture.

The gold standard would actually not completely ensure *internal* price stability, that is the stability of prices quoted in dollars, marks, or yen within each country. If for some reason, say technical change, the supply of goods in general were to increase faster than the supply of gold, prices expressed in gold would actually have to fall (unless offset by some increase in the velocity of circulation). Similarly, major gold discoveries, as did in fact happen at the end of the nineteenth century in the Klondike and South Africa, would logically cause the prices of other goods in terms of gold to increase. In the well-documented case of the USA, for example, there was indeed a deflation (falling prices) in the late nineteenth century. According to some statistics reprinted by McCallum (1989), wholesale (as opposed to consumer) prices fell by almost one-half (49 per cent) in the 1873–96 period.[4] Thereafter, presumably due to the gold discoveries of the later 1890s, prices began to rise again. From a somewhat longer-term perspective, however, prices would still be expected to be stable. It actually was the case that wholesale prices on average in the USA in 1910 were almost exactly the same as they had been 30 years earlier, in 1880. It would be this type of experience (what goes up must come down, or rather vice versa) which would ultimately mould general attitudes to what would be regarded as normal levels of prices under a gold standard regime.

The question of how the real economy (output, employment, growth) performed during periods in which prices were either stable or actually falling is a matter of considerable dispute. Traditionally, in the social and political histories, the period at the end of the nineteenth century was regarded as a period of considerable economic stagnation and distress in the advanced industrial economies such as Britain and the USA. In the USA, for example, the 1873–96 period was originally known as the 'Great Depression', before that title was usurped by what we now regard as the true Great Depression in 1929–33. In Britain, the decade of the 1880s, in particular, was certainly regarded as a period of social unrest, with the threat of actual revolution not far from the surface. Such episodes as the 'Black Monday' and 'Bloody Sunday' riots of the unemployed in 1886 and 1887, and the bitter dockers' strike later in the decade, would seem to illustrate the general atmosphere. It is well known that there was political unrest in the USA, also, at around the same time. This centred on the distress that falling prices were causing to groups such as farmers. For them the real burden of mortgages and the financing of working capital would continually be increasing, while the price of their actual produce would be continually falling. There was therefore agitation to revive the Civil War fiat currency or 'greenbacks', and also, most famously, to restore the free coinage of silver which had been abandoned in the 'Crime of 1873' (McCallum, 1989: 321). This agitation culminated in the US Presidential candidacies of William Jennings Bryan in 1896 and 1900, the first of which was notable for the famous 'cross of gold speech' at the Democratic party convention:[5]

> You shall not press down upon the brow of labor this crown of thorns, you shall not crucify mankind upon a cross of gold.

Bryan was not successful in his attempts to gain the White House, however, and a plausible explanation for this was that he was actually undone by the gold discoveries of the 1890s, as mentioned above. Prices began to rise again soon after 1896, taking the wind out of Bryan's sails.

As against the traditional picture of economic stagnation, however, more recent work by economic statisticians has convinced some economists that the story of the 'Great Depression' is a myth (Selgin, 1990: 65). For example, McCallum (1989: 321) points out that according to the latest estimates available at his time of writing there was a healthy rate of real GDP growth over the whole period 1870–1900. If so, this could be interpreted as evidence in favour of the long-run neoclassical 'natural rate' hypothesis according to which the behaviour of the real economy is independent of the behaviour of nominal variables such as nominal prices.

There has been some rewriting of history in this respect in the standard textbooks in recent years. One example is the difference between the first edition (1984) and the third edition (1990) of the well-known text by Barro. The first edition reports major recessions in the USA in 1873–75, 1882–85, 1893–94 and 1896, and an unemployment rate above 20 per cent in 1893–94 (Barro, 1984: 3, 6). By the third edition, however, in changes based largely on the work of Romer (for example, 1986a and 1986b) which had appeared in the meantime, only the 1893–94 recession remained. Even this was now reported as much less severe than before. The maximum unemployment reported was now only around 11 per cent. It is not quite clear how this new view squares with the political history or the reported views of people writing at the time. One possibility is that some groups, such as the farmers and other debtors, and also the participants in secularly declining industries, were indeed suffering, even if others were not, and that the voices of the former dominated the political debate (McCallum, 1989: 321; Selgin, 1990: 65–7).

Friedman and Friedman (1980: 3) have perhaps gone furthest in describing the gold standard world, with an effective world currency, rough price stability, and *laissez-faire* in public policy, as a 'golden age'.[6] On the other hand, as argued by Smithin (1985), if this was so, it is somewhat incongruous that the ultimate denouement of the period was World War I. It is difficult to accept that economic factors, such as the struggle for markets, played no part in the causes of the conflict.

Another reservation about the gold standard era, expressed by Hicks (1986: 21–2), was that in practice, far from being an automatic mechanism smoothly regulating the economic relations between nations, the operation of the system actually relied very heavily on the special place occupied by Britain, more specifically the Bank of England, in the economic order of the day. Given that the value of most of the world's currencies was fixed in gold, this should have meant, in principle, that the monetary authorities in each country were capable of paying out gold on demand in exchange for the national currency, to whatever extent was necessary. But, in reality, there was never actually enough gold in existence for this to be feasible. The working of the system therefore depended in an important way on the presence of a substitute for gold, which was thought to be 'as good as gold' but was more readily available. This was precisely the part paid by the pound sterling, that is the liabilities of the Bank of England. Confidence in the pound sterling, in turn, depended on the Bank of England itself being ready to pay out gold when required, and even more importantly on the economic strength of Britain itself. The simple fact that Britain was the major economic power of the day, and in particular was a creditor rather than a debtor nation, was what ultimately lay behind the strength of the pound.

The decline and impoverishment of Britain as a result of World War I, and particularly the change from debtor to creditor status, would therefore automatically mean that it would not be possible to reconstruct the international economic system after 1918 on the same basis as before. Much of the tortured economic and monetary history of the past 80 years can actually be traced back to this historical circumstance. In Hicks's words (1986: 22):

...the monetary history of this century – the world monetary history – all hangs together. It has gone on being a problem of finding something, in the world economy, which could play the part that was played by London before 1914.

THE IMPACT OF WORLD WAR I AND THE CHAOS OF THE INTERWAR PERIOD

If there is still academic dispute about the impact on the real economy of the deflationary bias of the pre-1914 gold standard, there is little or none about the deflation which occur' ', and the deflationary policies which were pursued, in the years between the two world wars, culminating in the 'true' Great Depression of the 1930s. Temin (1989) attributes this disaster also to the influence of the old gold standard, not directly, but because of the hold which the gold standard *ideology*, and the traditional ideas of sound finance, exerted on the minds of the leading policymakers and economists. They were thus led to advocate, and put into practice, monetary and macroeconomic policies which were catastrophically ill-suited to the conditions of the time. This story is particularly chilling from our contemporary perspective, because an analogous set of ideas has once again become the orthodox opinion of our own day, and is proclaimed in both the print and electronic media on a daily basis.

The gold standard, as such, was suspended by most of the major European belligerents shortly after the outbreak of World War I. That is to say that the relevant central banks were relieved of their formal obligations to redeem their liabilities in gold. Evidently, the usually constraining ideas of sound finance go out of the window whenever there is a war to be fought. Whatever needs to be done to provide the necessary resources *is* done in a way which is apparently unthinkable in peacetime. Embarrassingly from the point of view of orthodox economics, this is why wars are invariably associated with an economic boom domestically, whatever other horrors they may bring as they continue. Only the USA, which did not enter the war until 1917, stayed on the gold standard. Even in this case there was still upward pressure on prices as the world's gold flowed in to what was now obviously regarded as a safe haven compared to anywhere in Europe.

The main point about the suspension of the gold standard, however, was that for almost all the players concerned it was quite explicitly regarded as a temporary wartime measure, and it was thought that it would be possible to return to what had been regarded as normalcy as soon as the conflict was over. In the case of Britain, which had been the lynchpin of the pre-war system, the pound was allowed to 'float', in principle, for the first few years after the war. However, a decision was taken at a very early stage, following the report of the Cunliffe Committee of 1919, that the ultimate objective of policy was for the pound to be eventually returned to the gold standard at the pre-1914 parity of $4.86 to the pound. Under the spell of the then-current ideas about what constituted a sound basis for the currency, it was felt that this was the only course of action which could restore lasting prosperity. It did the opposite in practice.

A major difficulty in the ultimately futile attempt to restore the gold standard in the 1920s was the fact that inflation, once unleashed in World War I, had proceeded at very different rates in different countries. For example, prices had risen approximately 250 per cent in France, 150 per cent in Britain, and 'only' 100 per cent in the USA between 1914 and 1918. For Britain, for example, to return to the gold standard at the old parity, assuming prices in the USA now stayed the same, would require domestic prices to fall on average by around 20 per cent. This could only be achieved by the pursuit of deflationary 'tight money' policies, which would tend to raise the real interest rate, slow economic growth and thereby persuade the price and wage-setters in the economy, out of necessity, to accept the cuts. Accordingly, this was the route that Britain took in the 1920s, with the result that the economy was sluggish and the unemployment rate high throughout the decade.

The *coup de grâce* occurred in 1925, when the then Chancellor, Winston Churchill, finally made the announcement that Britain would go back on the gold standard at the old parity. It was obviously felt that the several years of sacrifice had accomplished their objective, and that the value of the pound had risen sufficiently to be within striking distance of the old parity. Unfortunately, as Keynes pointed out in his famous pamphlet *The Economic Consequences of Mr. Churchill* (1925), the new parity *still* overvalued the pound by approximately 10 per cent in the conditions of 1925. In essence then, what was now required to restore British competitiveness was an all-round wage cut of around 10 per cent. The response of the labour unions to this led directly to the massive industrial unrest which culminated in the General Strike of 1926, and poor economic performance for the next several years. Eventually, the strain became too much, and Britain was forced off the gold standard and allowed the pound to float during the world financial crisis of 1931. This was perceived as a political disaster at the time, and it finally finished off whatever hopes Britain may have had of returning the City of London to the prestigious position it had occupied before 1914. Nonetheless, from the point of view of the domestic British economy, the move was actually beneficial, as British goods would now be more competitive on world markets. In principle, there was now nothing standing in the way of expansionary domestic macroeconomic policy. As a matter of fact, Temin (1989: 3–4) points out that in relative terms the British economy did not fare as badly as some others (such as the USA and Wiemar Germany) in the Depression of the 1930s. However, the policy authorities did not take full advantage of the opportunity offered them, presumably due to a lingering commitment to fiscal and monetary orthodoxy.

The USA, meanwhile, had a very different 1920s than did Britain. The so-called 'Jazz Age' was actually a time of some prosperity (Sekine, 1993: 1).[7] This was complacently recounted by President Hoover in his notoriously ill-timed State of the Union Address in 1928 (Galbraith, 1994: 58). Evidently, the US equivalent of a central bank, the Federal Reserve System, which had only been in existence since 1913, had been doing an adequate job in managing the nation's money in its early years (Friedman and Friedman, 1980: 78). However, as is well known, the Fed has also been accused of later being a major culprit in both provoking and prolonging the Depression of the 1930s. The first scholars to make this charge were Friedman and Schwartz in their famous work *A Monetary History of the United States* (1963). In their view, the Great Depression was not caused by the 1929 stock market crash *per se* (this was just a symptom[8]) but by a perverse response of the Federal Reserve System to the crisis. They note that the money supply was allowed to fall by as much as one-third between 1929 and 1933. This led to a banking crisis (exacerbated by the weaknesses of the US banking system at that time), and, through familiar arguments about the short-run effect of monetary policy on real output, to the Depression.

Temin (1989) also blames deflationary policy in the USA, by *both* the monetary and fiscal authorities, for the Depression in that country, but unlike Friedman and Schwartz would lay the ultimate blame on the gold standard ideology which was still exerting a baleful influence on the ideas of policymakers and practitioners. It did so in two ways, first in seeming to mandate deflationary policy in the late 1920s, in the case of the USA in an attempt to slow down the stock market boom (which succeeded only too well); second, in seeming to indicate that still *further* deflation was the appropriate policy response to the problems of the 1930s (Temin, 1989: 42). Temin stresses, in particular, the impact of the expectation of continued deflation on real interest rates, the so-called 'Mundell effect' (Mundell, 1963). High real rates, in turn, provoked the economic decline (Temin, 1989: 56–7).

Deflationism had a still more devastating effect in Germany, when, under the Bruning administration in 1930–32 it generated over seven million unemployed, and played a major role in generating the discontent which brought Hitler to power in 1933 (Galbraith, 1994: 81). Once again, it might well be argued that the ideology of the gold standard and of so-called sound finance was to blame. Germany had not been on the gold standard, of course, during the hyperinflation of 1922/23, and that earlier episode was apparently a major influence on the attitude of establishment policymakers a decade later. One factor was that among the conditions of the international agreement by which the German crisis of the 1920s was resolved was a requirement that Germany should return to the paths of financial orthodoxy (Temin, 1989: 18). Equally important was the lingering psychological impact of the memories of the hyperinflation. The later policymakers were desperately afraid of doing anything at all which might conceivably rekindle inflationary pressures (Temin, 1989: 63).

Ironically, the situation of France, the remaining major protagonist of the 1919 Versailles Peace Conference, in the 1920s and 1930s, was the mirror image of that of Britain. In the words of Temin (1989: 18), 'France refused to accept the burden of deflation...' . When it did eventually go back on gold it was with the franc valued at one-fifth of its pre-war level. Thus, the franc was undervalued rather than overvalued during the 1920s, with commensurate benefits for the French economy. However, having gone back on gold, France then maintained the standard in the changed circumstances of the 1930s for much longer than did Britain. The result was that the franc then became *overvalued* during the Depression, and economic conditions greatly worsened (Temin, 1989: 77).

Hicks (1982: 276) makes some attempt to explain these typical attitudes of the 1920s and 1930s, by quoting Robertson, writing at the time, as follows:

> Our economic order is largely based upon the institution of contract – on the fact, that is, that people enter into binding agreements with one another to perform certain actions at a future date, for remuneration which is fixed here and now in terms of money. A violent or prolonged change in the value of money saps the confidence with which people accept or make undertakings of this nature.

Hicks points out that it was natural for Robertson, in the 1920s, to think in these terms. The great inflations following World War I were still fresh in the memory, and these had followed the long Victorian era of virtual price stability. In such circumstances, Robertson's comments, and the policy recommendations which would follow from them, are at least understandable. It is less understandable, however, that similar attitudes should prevail or be revived in the late twentieth century, among populations who have had far more experience of inflationary conditions. As Hicks has noted, what Robertson's argument, viewed as a general proposition, seems to require is not so much price stability *per se* but *predictability*. If the inflation rate was consistently around 10 per cent, say, and this was expected to continue, there would be no problem in entering into nominal contracts which take this into account. Similarly, if it could always be guaranteed that the real return on financial assets would be positive, regardless of the rate at which they were depreciating in nominal terms, there would be no disincentive for the accumulation of such assets in the course of economic activity. Ironically, Robertson's argument could actually be used *against* the stringent disinflationary policies of the last quarter of the twentieth century. In these circumstances, inflation had previously become entrenched and a large proportion of nominal contracts and economic planning generally had been based on the assumption that it was going to continue.

THE BRETTON WOODS ERA AND POSTWAR PROSPERITY

After the disasters of the interwar period, there was clearly some determination on the part of those responsible for post-World War II reconstruction that the mistakes of the earlier period should not be repeated. There was no question this time of any attempt to return to pre-war normalcy. There had been no normalcy to begin with. As it turned out, the economic regime prevailing in the advanced industrialized nations in the third quarter of the twentieth century is now looked back on as a halcyon period of relatively rapid growth and full employment. It may not be quite correct to describe this period as the heyday of 'Keynesian economics', because it is now clear that the original ideas of Keynes (1936) were subject to substantial misunderstanding and misinterpretation by the leading academics and politicians of the day. Nonetheless, whether due to the influence of Keynes or otherwise, the so-called Keynesian policies seemed to have nothing but success for the first 30 to 35 years after the publication of Keynes's book. Within a short space of time, the impact of government spending on the economy during World War II seemed to provide what Galbraith (1987: 237–65) has called 'affirmation by Mars'. When war broke out in Europe in 1939, the economies of Britain and North America were still seriously depressed, but within a short space of time full employment was very easily restored under the stimulus of the enforced massive increase in the activities of the state. That of Germany had already recovered thanks to Hitler's own preparations for war. Nobody (presumably) would have used this experience to argue that war is a good thing. It would clearly be a very different matter for those countries on whose territory the carnage was actually occurring, than in the USA or Canada. Nonetheless, the economic spin-offs of the conflict would naturally lead on to the thought that if government spending for war-like ends could produce such a result, then something similar might later be achieved by spending for more peaceful purposes. By the end of the war, such a philosophy had indeed permeated official thinking; finding expression, for example, in the Employment Act of 1946 in the USA (Tobin, 1986a). The following 25 years or so, down to the early 1970s, during which the supposedly 'Keynesian' policies were in vogue, were an era which seems in retrospect a remarkable period of economic prosperity for the capitalist economies. In most jurisdictions, the performance in terms of growth, productivity and employment would compare very favourably with the most successful periods in each nation's history, and certainly with either the 1930s or the stagnant period of the 1970s which followed. The business cycle itself seemed to contemporary observers to have been substantially tamed. The title of a well-received volume of research papers published at the time (Brofenbrenner, 1969) was *Is the Business Cycle Obsolete?*. Even if the answer given by most of the period researchers was a cautious 'no', the fact that the question could be asked at all is indicative of the general mood. It was suggested that the characteristics of the postwar business cycle had been greatly modified. Business cycles were now much milder and shorter, and recessions now tended to be 'growth recessions', in which all that occurred was a slowing down of the *rate* of growth, rather than the catastrophic falls in output of the 1930s.

Evidently this situation was satisfactory not only to labour, who benefited from full employment and rising real wages, but also to business, in the sense of manufacturers and producers, as business profits are more buoyant in periods of prosperity rather than depression. The financial interests, who in the past would have favoured such regimes as the old-fashioned gold stand-ard, would be less enamoured of the new situation, but the unique compro-mise between the competing economic interests nonetheless held for at least two decades.

During the Bretton Woods era of 'fixed but adjustable' exchange rates, world monetary policy would be primarily determined by that of the major player, the US Federal Reserve System. In a sense, monetary policy was relegated to playing primarily a supporting role. Interest rates were kept relatively low and stable, certainly by later standards. From the point of view of the financial sector, however, the regime was apparently acceptable as long as *real* returns continued to be positive and the value of financial wealth was at least maintained. It was true that there was persistent inflation through most of the period of prosperity, even though, again, this was mild by later standards. However, real returns remained positive. Therefore, even if the rate of return to financial instruments was not large, the owners of such assets were at least protected from the erosion of the real value of their capital. The 'Keynesian' or full employment regime therefore gained a provisional acqui-escence, even if not an enthusiastic welcome, from this quarter.

There is, however, a school of thought which attributes the prosperity of the postwar period not to any Keynesian-type domestic macroeconomic poli-cies in individual countries, but to a benign external environment, specifically the Bretton Woods system of fixed but adjustable exchanges rates itself. Also, the growing liberalization of world trade under the auspices of the GATT (General Agreement on Tariffs and Trade). Keynes himself was one of the architects of the new international system at the original 1944 conference in

Bretton Woods, New Hampshire, but this is not what is usually meant by Keynesian economics.

From the point of view of Hicks's 'world monetary history', the purpose of the Bretton Woods agreement was to reintroduce some semblance of stability to the system, which had apparently been lost with the demise of the old gold standard in 1914. Since then stability had not been restored, in spite of the various futile attempts to do so in the interwar period.

The Bretton Woods system was not really a new gold standard. Only one currency, the US dollar, was exchangeable for gold, at $35 per ounce, and even this privilege was extended only to the monetary authorities of other nations, not to the general public. All other countries would use one of the 'key currencies', that is the national currency of one of the major players, as the medium in which to hold their international reserves. In effect, the most important key currency was now the US dollar, although a 'face-saving' role for the pound sterling was maintained in theory, at least until the devaluation of 1967. Clearly, if the operation of the old gold standard had depended in practice on the policy of the Bank of England, the 'world central bank' in the immediate postwar world was the US Federal Reserve System. As Hicks (1986) has pointed out, the well-known network of international financial institutions (IFIs) set up at Bretton Woods, such as the IMF and the World Bank, was largely a facade which only slightly obscured the reality. The system was never as rigid as the gold standard had been. It was always allowable for the exchange rates to be adjusted (usually devalued) from time to time, in the case of an ill-defined 'fundamental disequilibrium'. This latter possibility was productive of numerous old-fashioned financial crises throughout the period.

In the end, the Bretton Woods system remained in place for more than two decades down to August 1971, when President Nixon finally cut the link between the US dollar and gold, removing the formal underpinnings of what had been effectively a US dollar standard. By early 1973, all the main currencies were floating against one another, and the non-system of the last quarter of the twentieth century, the managed or 'dirty' float, was in place.

It is striking, of course, that the Bretton Woods era did coincide almost exactly with the postwar period of macroeconomic stability and prosperity. This in itself, possibly in combination with a somewhat rosy and nostalgic view of the old gold standard period, has been enough to lead many observers to conclude that the system of fixed exchange rates was actually the *cause* of the favourable performance. Some such feeling, combined with the apparent volatility of the foreign exchange markets in the 1980s and 1990s, is no doubt behind the contemporary enthusiasm in some quarters for a return to some type of fixed exchange rate system – a 'new Bretton Woods'. This, however, is a question on which it is crucial to separate cause and effect. It is probably

closer to the truth that whatever the exchange rate system, it is the macroeconomic policies of the major players, the most important economic powers,
which set the tone for prosperity or depression. The stability or otherwise of
the foreign exchanges emerges simultaneously as a by-product. In the Bretton
Woods era, obviously, the major player was the USA, and as long as American policies were consistent with both economic expansion and with maintaining the dollar's pivotal role in the international monetary system (a deli-
cate balancing act) the Bretton Woods system could hold *and* the world
economy could be relatively prosperous. When American policy actions failed
to fulfil both conditions, however, both the exchange rate system and world
prosperity collapsed. Equally, a coherent set of macroeconomic policies by
the main players could presumably make a nominally floating exchange rate
system work reasonably well. In other words, a large part of the responsibility for the instability of exchange rates observed in practice at the end of the
twentieth century can be laid at the door of unintelligent policy. Temin (1989:
38) has made a similar point with respect to the earlier period between the
wars, as discussed above:

> [This] view...reverses a traditional conclusion of international economics. Con-
> temporary observers drew from the interwar experience the conclusion that floating
> exchange rates lead to economic chaos...They correctly observed the correlation,
> but they reversed the causation. It was actually that economic instability leads to
> floating exchange rates.

As far as the collapse of Bretton Woods is concerned, the critics of Keynesian
economics would no doubt have argued that some sort of reckoning was
ultimately inevitable. It was always argued that there was a downside to
Keynesian policies in terms of undesirable side-effects such as budget deficits and inflation. Indeed, the prevalence of such symptoms in more recent
history is often popularly portrayed as simply the legacy of these earlier
times, in spite of the strained chronology that such a view entails. Interestingly enough, however, this downside was actually *not* particularly noticeable
during the prosperous postwar era. In the USA between 1948 and 1970, for
example, the annual average inflation rate (measured by the consumer price
index) was only around 2.5 per cent. It is true that to a population accustomed
to either price stability or declining prices, even this low rate would have
been regarded as high at the time. By later standards, however, this was an
extraordinarily successful inflation performance. Similarly, the US federal
government budget was balanced or in surplus in seven out of 23 years
between 1948 and 1970, and the annual average budgetary deficit was only
–0.3 per cent of GNP. Only in a couple of years, notably fiscal 1959 and fiscal
1968, was the budget deficit at a level anything like comparable to that of
later years, with deficits in those two instances approaching 3 per cent of

GNP. In other jurisdictions, the numbers on budget deficits and inflation, even if different in the details, would also be similarly encouraging by later standards. There is remarkably little evidence from this early period to support the view that the inevitable cost of full-employment policies is budget deficits and chronic inflation. At the very least, the economies of the industrialized democracies were able to 'get away with it' for around two-and-a-half decades.

THE STAGFLATION OF THE 1970s

Severe problems, or at least problems which were widely perceived as severe at the time, did appear, of course, after the break-up of the Bretton Woods system in the early 1970s. One of these was simply that double-digit inflation did finally emerge as an apparently intractable issue. Even worse, to the conventional way of thinking, was the emergence of the new phenomenon of 'stagflation'. By this time it had become generally accepted that inflation, unemployment and the business cycle were related by a rough 'Phillips-curve'[9] type of relationship. Inflation would tend to accelerate during the boom when unemployment was low, and to ease in a recessionary phase when growth was stagnant and unemployment was rising. Confidence in this relationship was severely weakened during the 1970s, when, in what seemed like the worst of all possible worlds, recessions and periods of low growth were actually accompanied by *rising* inflation.

The most common interpretation of these difficulties would be that the policies of the previous 25 years had failed, and even that they were responsible for the new situation. Needless to say, however, this is not the view of the self-described 'Keynesian' economists who presided over policymaking in the postwar era. For example, members of the distinguished group who were members of the US Council of Economic Advisors (CEA) during the Kennedy and Johnson administrations, still believe that the standard demand management policies worked well enough in their day. They would further argue that the inflation and stagflation of the 1970s, and the collapse of Bretton Woods, were all actually caused by a *failure* to apply the approved Keynesian remedies. In this scenario, the crucial issue was the prevarication by the US government over the financing of the Vietnam War in the late 1960s. On orthodox Keynesian principles, increased spending during wartime is in itself enough to provoke a boom in the domestic economy.[10] Hence, the economic problem during wartime, assuming the fighting is not actually on domestic soil, is to prevent the economy from overheating and causing the usual wartime inflation. To prevent this, President Johnson's Keynesian advisors, were, by their own account, urging a tax increase as early as 1965, arguing that if the wartime expenditures were tax financed this would dampen inflationary pressures. Vietnam, however, was an extremely unpopular war, and the President was unwilling to raise taxes. Nothing was done until 1968, by which time, according to the late Walter W. Heller (1986: 6–7), the former CEA chair, 'the inflation horse was out of the barn'. The argument of the US Keynesians in other words is that against their advice the Vietnam War was largely money-financed, and that this led to inflation.

The argument would then continue that rising domestic prices then led to a loss of competitiveness abroad and balance of payments problems, culminating in the severing of the link between the dollar and gold by Johnson's successor Nixon in 1971, and the collapse of the Bretton Woods system. On this view, therefore, it was the Vietnam War inflation which was responsible for sinking Bretton Woods and for the spread of inflationary pressures around the world. However, this was alleged to be not the result of Keynesian policy, but actually of *not* following basic Keynesian principles. The actual stagflation episodes of the 1970s, as things seemed to go from bad to worse, would then be blamed on the two OPEC (Organization of Petroleum Exporting Countries) 'oil shocks' which hit the industrialized nations in 1973 and 1979. After all, it is simply a matter of basic economic principle that reductions in supply lead to lower output with higher prices.

With the benefit of hindsight, and also with the objective of explaining subsequent political developments, it can also be argued that the most salient feature of the 'stagflationary' decade of the 1970s, ending the era of postwar optimism, was really neither just the emergence of more severe inflationary pressures, nor even the unusual combination of the latter with sluggish or negative growth. More particularly, it was the initial response of the monetary authorities to the various shocks, which effectively abandoned the original compromise between the competing economic interests. In the course of the monetary policy response, real rates of return on financial instruments in many jurisdictions were allowed to fall very low, and actually became negative at times. Thus for the first time the financial interests were directly threatened. After the collapse of Bretton Woods and the floating of exchange rates, it would no longer be the case that US policy alone was dictating world developments. However, both in the USA and elsewhere, and with different proximate reasons depending on short-run political developments in each case, the initial emphasis was on a continuation of easy money policies. The motivation was presumably to deal with stagnating output and employment, but the result was that the owners of financial capital failed to receive the protection from the inflationary aspects of the new situation to which they felt entitled. It was this, plausibly, that then led to strong pressure, emanating from the financial interests, for the 'change in monetary regime' which did in fact occur in the late 1970s and early 1980s.

'BACK TO THE FUTURE'? THE FINANCIAL REACTION IN THE LAST QUARTER OF THE TWENTIETH CENTURY

There were actually three highly symbolic harbingers of the political revolution that was to come during the crucial year of 1979. One such was the much-publicized change in the operating procedures of the US Fed, after the appointment of a new chair, Paul Volcker, who was very much the candidate of the financial markets (Greider, 1987). There ensued a three-year effort to bring inflation down via monetary tightness and high real rates of interest. This did ultimately succeed in its objective, but only at the cost of a severe recession in 1981/82, with the unemployment rate reaching the 10 per cent range.

Also in 1979, the most famous adherent of monetarism among politicians, Margaret Thatcher, was elected to her first term as British Prime Minister, and in the next year her government began a similarly draconian disinflation policy, the so-called 'medium term financial strategy' (MTFS).

Finally, perhaps less-remarked at the time than the first two events, but of equal significance in hindsight, the year 1979 also saw the inauguration of the European Monetary System (EMS), and the associated exchange rate mechanism (ERM). The objective was initially to reduce, and later to eliminate, exchange rate variability between the main currencies of the then European Community (now the EU). In the future, this would ensure that pan-European monetary policy would be determined essentially by the German Bundesbank, which, because of previous history, was an institution traditionally committed to the type of hardline anti-inflation policy which became very much the order of the day in the 1980s and 1990s.

From around 1979–82 on, there was a perceptible change in the attitudes of policymakers, leading academics, and those shaping opinion such as financial journalists. There was a rejection of the previous Keynesian-type attitudes to macroeconomic policy, with their stress on maintaining the pressure of aggregate demand, cheap money, full employment, etc. The focus changed to concern with the types of monetary and financial variables which are usually of interest to financial investors such as bondholders. Inflation was now seen as a matter of primary concern, as was the nominal value of the exchange rate in each jurisdiction, and later the nominal or money value of the government budget deficit. From the historical point of view, this could be regarded as something of a reversion to the attitudes and psychological values of a previous era, as described above.

The 'change in monetary regime' occurring in the late 1970s and early 1980s, and which in spirit (if not in terms of precise operating procedures) has persisted into the 1990s, certainly seemed to succeed in terms of its declared objective. Parkin (1994: 2), for example, summarizes the inflation experience of the G7 countries as follows:

severe inflation began in almost all countries during the early 1970s and persisted through the rest of that decade and into the [early] 1980s...during the 1980s inflation declined and by the early 1990s it had returned to a similar level to that of the early 1960s...the experience of individual countries follows the same broad pattern...Germany has generally experienced lower than average inflation, the United Kingdom and Italy have persistently inflated faster than average, the United States, Canada, and France have performed close to the average and Japan...[had] ...above average [inflation] before 1975...[and]...below average since 1975.

In addition, the new regime clearly did succeed in restoring the value of financial capital and in raising the real rate of return earned on that capital. However, this was at the expense of real returns to both labour and the non-financial business sector, and to the detriment of real economic performance. There were serious recessions in many jurisdictions in both the early 1980s and early 1990s (in 1981/82 and 1990/91 in North America) and mass unemployment became a serious problem again in many parts of the world, really for the first time since the 1930s. In the first half of the 1990s, for example, annual average unemployment rates were more than 10 per cent in both the EU and Canada, and around 7 per cent in the USA.[11] There seemed to be a substantial element of 'overkill' in the process of disinflation, in the sense that the political goals were articulated obliquely in terms of permanently lower or 'zero' inflation, rather than simply preserving the value of accumulated financial wealth by ensuring that real financial returns remain positive. Actual experience seems to indicate that it is extraordinarily difficult, in contemporary capitalist economies, to get the inflation down close to zero and keep it there, without severe negative side-effects in terms of depressed output and mass unemployment. This in spite of what textbook models with expectations-augmented Phillips curves and natural rates of unemployment would suggest. In technical language, at the very least the processes involved seem to be subject to substantial degrees of hysteresis and/or persistence.

There were at least two identifiable phases of the fight against inflation in the 1980s and 1990s. The first was the period of the 'monetarist experiments' (Smithin, 1990: 34–55) of the early 1980s, when central banks around the world announced their conversion to a more-or-less Friedmanite version of monetarism and attempted to tame inflation by sticking to strict monetary growth 'targets'. This targeting *per se* was actually a failure, wherever it was tried, largely because the period was also one of fairly rapid financial innovation in which the traditional definitions of the 'money supply' were rapidly becoming obsolete. On the other hand, inflation certainly *was* brought under control and everywhere fell very rapidly from the heights it had reached in the late 1970s. In practice, this was achieved by driving up real interest rates and thus provoking an economic slowdown severe enough to 'discipline' those involved in the price-setting and wage-bargaining process.

Economies around the world then began to recover in the late 1980s, due to a combination of easing of interest rates after 1982, and, it must be said, President Reagan's inadvertent 'Keynesian' policy of fiscal stimulus in the USA, following tax cuts initiated in his first term of office (Smithin, 1990: 61–5). Almost as soon as economic activity began to recover however, inflation rates (not surprisingly from a common-sense point of view) began to creep up again. There was therefore a series of further policy-induced recessions in the early 1990s, justified on the grounds that it was now necessary to slow down an 'overheating' economy in order to head off the potential threat of inflation once again. Indeed, attitudes to inflation had actually seemed to harden from those of the early 1980s, and many policymakers now proclaimed that their ultimate goal was zero inflation or literal price stability. There was very little talk of monetary targeting this time round, however, and central banks seemed to revert in practice to their traditional interest rate and exchange rate focus. It was now much more explicitly a case of simply driving up interest rates in order to reduce the pace of economic activity. Inflation rates did come down once more to historically low levels, as indicated in the quote from Parkin, but again at the cost of substantial increases in unemployment. Later there was another recovery (which was fairly vigorous in the USA, if not elsewhere), but already through 1994 and into 1995 the main topic of discussion for observers of monetary policy was once again the need to raise interest rates to head off the threat of inflation.

The Canadian experience in the 1980s and 1990s was in many ways a microcosm of what was occurring on the world stage. Two specific episodes in which the fight against inflation apparently destabilized the real economy immediately come to mind. The first would be the later years of the monetary targeting experiment of 1975–82. In this case the original Canadian policy of 'gradualism' was drastically intensified by an attempted defence of the exchange rate at the very time that the US Federal Reserve was itself pursuing a hardline policy of disinflation (Courchene, 1982). This did lead to a lower Canadian inflation rate in the mid-1980s but at the cost of a severe recession in 1981/82 and an annual average unemployment rate which remained in double figures through 1985. The second episode would be the 'zero inflation' policy announced by the then-Governor of the Bank of Canada, John Crow, in 1988 (Lipsey, 1990; McLean and Osberg, forthcoming; McQuaig, 1995). Once again, high real interest rates were the vehicle for inducing disinflation, and, because on this occasion the Canadian policy was *more* drastic than comparable initiatives in the USA, currency appreciation also. The recession of the early 1990s was distinctive in being a 'made-in-Canada' product in this sense. As early as 1992, the policy might have been judged to be a success in the sense that the inflation rate had fallen to below 2 per cent in that year (Smithin, forthcoming). However, the price to be paid was the renewed recession of 1990/91, and a national unemployment rate that had climbed back into double figures by 1991 and remained in that range through the early 1990s. Moreover, Canada apparently received very little credit from the international financial community for the pain and suffering which its citizens had suffered in the battle to get the inflation rate down. As early as 1994, when the USA (which had not reduced inflation as much as the Canadians) began to raise interest rates again, the Canadian dollar fell and the Bank of Canada felt obliged to follow, regardless of its hard-fought victory on the inflation front. Zero inflation was now apparently worth nothing in the eyes of the international investors.

In addition to the objective of zero inflation, whose purpose is obviously to maintain the *internal* value of the currency, the preoccupation of many policymakers in the 1990s with the *external* value of their nation's currency has had a similarly old-world flavour reminiscent of the gold standard days. A classic example here was surely Britain's belated entry to the ERM in Europe at overvalued par value for the pound in 1990. There were apparently at least two motivating factors for the authorities to take this disastrous step. First, the desire on the part of some members of the British establishment to demonstrate their credentials as 'good Europeans' in the context of the movement towards European economic integration and the eventual plans for a common European currency. Second, the more traditional objective of maintaining monetary discipline and avoiding inflation. A popular argument at this time was that if the major player in a fixed exchange rate system was perceived to be committed to low inflation and monetary discipline, while the domestic authorities were not, the necessary restraint could be imported by the requirement to maintain a fixed exchange rate. In the specific case of British ERM membership, the policies of the German Bundesbank were seen as having been responsible for a low average inflation rate within the ERM, and the ERM itself for the apparent convergence of inflation rates among members. On the other hand, British social and political arrangements, such as the wage bargaining system and the lack of political independence of the Bank of England were widely seen as being incapable on their own of delivering an inflation rate to match those prevalent in continental Europe.

For those in favour of entry to the ERM, the short-term political solution was to 'tie the hands' of the monetary authorities by ERM membership, relying on the defence of the exchange rate to impose anti-inflationary discipline. The longer-term solution would be to remove the monetary policy debate from the British political arena altogether, by submitting to a currency union and the policy of a supra-national central bank. In the event, Britain's short-lived ERM membership of 1990–92 appears in every respect to have been a replay of the return to gold in 1925–31. There was a similar deliberate deflation of the domestic economy both before and after the event, and a similar professed helplessness of the authorities to deal with the resulting unemployment because of the constraints imposed by the defence of the exchange rate. Even the role of the 'City' and the financial press in agitating for the change, noted by Kaldor (1986) for the 1925 episode, was repeated in the 1980s and 1990s. The analogy with the 1925–31 episode seemed even more striking following the 'suspension' of Britain's membership after the financial crisis of September 1992, which also forced the Italian lira out of the system. As in 1931, this was perceived in orthodox circles as a political disaster, but from the economic point of view represented much needed relief from deflationary pressure imposed from the outside, specifically from the high interest rate policy pursued by the German Bundesbank in the wake of German unification.[12]

Mention of the Bundesbank also reminds us of another seemingly major change in the international economic environment of the late 1980s and 1990s. As has been remarked in the case of the waning economic power of Britain after 1914, the identity of the international reserve currencies, and hence world financial leadership in that sense, seems to be based on the most crude indicators of national economic success. Basically, a nation seems to be able to claim the central position if it has a large excess of net credits against outside nations on which it can potentially draw in times of need. As in the case of the pre-1914 UK, these may actually be denominated in the currency of the reserve centre itself, but they ultimately represent a claim against the real resources of other nations, built up by superior economic performance over time. Once a large credit position has been achieved, the point must be that any promises to pay issued on the security of that position become more trustworthy than those of any rival and will themselves be regarded by third parties as adequate payment for goods and services received. In the case of the UK, the move from creditor to debtor status after World War I would then account for its demise as the world financial centre. Britain was eventually replaced by the USA, but, notoriously, the USA itself became a debtor nation after 1985, and many observers also feel that this heralds an eventual changing of the guard in international finance. This may account for the recent apparent changes in the relative positions of the US dollar on the one hand, and the Japanese yen and German D-Mark on the other. The most popular view today is of a 'three-cornered' world in which no one currency has the old hegemonic power of Britain or the USA in their heyday, and international investors have to pay equal attention to developments in each of the three main blocs.

CONCLUSION

The overwhelming impression left by this, admittedly selective, survey of well over a century of macroeconomic history is that of *déjà vu*, or a wheel turning full circle. In the gold standard world described by Sir John Hicks, the main preoccupation of policymakers and commentators on economic events was obviously with such issues as price stability, maintaining the (gold) value of the currency, the principles of sound finance, and so on. The assumption, which may or may not have been valid in its own day, was presumably that if these things could be achieved, the real economy would take care of itself.

Remarkably, after all the twists and turns of macroeconomic history of the past 100 years, including a period of unprecedented prosperity during which some very different ideas gained at least a partial acceptance, the most accurate characterization of the main concerns of today's policymakers and leading academic economists would again be an exclusive focus on a very similar set of issues. The same history, however, would seem to provide at least some worrying evidence that these obsessions may well be counterproductive and even dangerous from the point of view of the real economy.

NOTES

1. IMF, *World Economic Outlook*, Washington, DC, May 1995.
2. Determined essentially by the physical transportation costs of gold.
3. That is, to discontinue the coinage of silver.
4. The USA had not been on a gold standard during the Civil War period, of course, and prices had risen dramatically in 1861–65. This may explain a considerable part of the subsequent fall.
5. As quoted by Mankiw (1992: 168). Mankiw goes on to make the fascinating observation that the supposed children's story *The Wizard of Oz* was originally actually an allegory about this episode in monetary history, the 'yellow brick road' representing the gold standard.
6. It is not obvious from the context whether the pun is intentional or not.
7. However, Sekine (1993: 2, 9–10) would argue that this prosperity was to some extent illusory, due to structural problems.
8. See also Smithin (1990: 109–23).
9. So called after a famous paper by Phillips (1958) which documented the relationship between wage inflation and unemployment in Britain over a period of nearly a century.
10. In the specific case of the USA in the 1960s, this impact would also be combined with increased domestic spending in connection with President Johnson's 'Great Society' programme.
11. IMF, *World Economic Outlook*, Washington, DC, May 1995.
12. In July/August 1993 another exchange rate crisis led to a dramatic widening of the permitted bands of fluctuation for the remaining ERM members.

3. Politics and economics

INTRODUCTION

A working title of this chapter was *Capitalism, Socialism, Fascism and Democracy*, which is a reference to the title of Schumpeter's famous book, *Capitalism, Socialism and Democracy* (1942; 1975) originally published in 1942. This work put forward the thesis that the capitalism of the day was decaying and would be replaced by some form of socialism. Such a view was widely held at the time, but was somewhat unusual in being put forward by someone who was actually a committed advocate of *laissez-faire* capitalism. The point of the reference was simply to draw attention to the inescapable connection between economics and politics.

It is a rather difficult task, however, to find a place for the ideas in this book along the contemporary political spectrum. This is due primarily to the dogmatism and rigidity with which economists typically present their political ideas. To be fair, this seems also to be a general cultural phenomenon. In the radically different field of what she calls 'sex studies', the American anti-establishment author and scholar Camille Paglia (1994: xviii) recently suggested that:

> a sterile liberal versus conservative debate has polarized the campuses and prevented authentic self-critique. These political propositions are simplistic and outmoded. We must take the best from the left and the best from the right to devise new strategies for the twenty-first century.

It is the contention of this chapter that if this is true of sex, arguably one of the two main objects of human preoccupation, it is equally so of the other, namely money.

THE DEBATE ABOUT THE MARKET MECHANISM

In the realm of economics, clearly the main debating points have been the extent to which commercial life should be organized on the basis of what is variously called capitalism or the market economy, and whether or not there is a connection between this type of economic system and liberal democracy

in politics. This is a debate which has been raging since at least the publication of Adam Smith's *Wealth of Nations* (1776; 1970) and presumably will
continue. However, in our own time the terms of the debate have been
drastically altered by the collapse of communism in central and Eastern
Europe, and the former Soviet Union, after 1989. One of the main alternative
systems on offer, which had fascinated political activists and intellectuals for
most of the present century, was demonstrated after all to be economically
and morally bankrupt in a most decisive fashion. Some commentators have
interpreted this as the final triumph, at least on the plain of ideas, of both
market capitalism and liberal democracy, as in Francis Fukayama's *The End
of History* (1992).

There are, however, at least two problems with this view. The first is that
the 1980s and 1990s, which were clearly disastrous economically for the
former communist states, were also not times of rampant economic prosperity in the West. In particular, the two worldwide recessions of the early 1980s
and early 1990s, and the return of levels of unemployment which would have
been unthinkable 20 years earlier, indicate that there are major problems
which remain to be solved. As mentioned, the widely-accepted doctrine that a
certain level of unemployment is absolutely necessary if inflation is to be
kept under control, has uncomfortable (if unconscious) echoes of Marx's
'reserve army of the unemployed'. The second point is that the mere fact that
socialism or communism has proven undesirable and collapsed, does not
actually deal with the issue of why these attempted solutions once seemed so
necessary to millions of people around the world. World War I and the Great
Depression were not figments of the imagination. Obviously it was their
occurrence which persuaded many that the existing system was not working
and needed to be changed. The question is how and whether a revived
laissez-faire capitalism could avoid similar catastrophes.

THE ROLE OF PRICE STABILITY AND DEFLATIONISM

The general set of ideas around price stability, zero inflation and the merits of
disinflation, are usually taken to be simply part and parcel of the overall
package of market-orientated reforms. The usual argument, as in the quotation from Robertson in chapter 2 above, is that price stability is simply a
prerequisite for the market economy to succeed. In actual fact, the economic
history of the last century seems to indicate that the opposite is rather closer
to the truth, at least in the sense that the various attempts to achieve stable
prices have often been damaging and that the most prosperous periods have
been those of mild inflation. Therefore the most committed advocates of the
market system in this respect, to the extent that their ideas do succeed in

being put into practice, are the ones most likely to cause serious political damage to their own ideals. There is an obvious historical example of this in the fate of Germany in the 1920s and 1930s. Note that Hitler did *not* achieve power as a result of the German hyperinflation of 1922/23, extreme though that episode was. The 'beer hall putsch' of 1923 was a failure and the Nazi leaders were jailed. By 1928 the National Socialists received only 2.6 per cent of the vote in national elections (Krieger, 1969). However, *after* the deflationary policies of the Bruning administration in 1930–32, and the mass unemployment that this entailed, it was a different story. The National Social-ist party actually received 37 per cent of the vote in the Reichstag election of 1932, and acquired the national position which later enabled them to seize power. The point, presumably, is that they were at least offering an alternative to the orthodox philosophy of despair and the attitude that nothing can be done.

In terms of actual results, therefore, so far from preserving the market system, what deflationism actually does is to trade-off a depressed overall economy for the benefit of a particular group. While not denying that this group must receive *some* reward if the capitalism system is to be viable at all, this situation is self-evidently not politically stable.

Something of the difficulty can be perceived by referring to a book of reminiscences by one of the leading free-market thinkers, Ludwig von Mises (1978), which was published a few years after his death, but actually written many years before. Mises was, of course, an influential member of the so-called 'Austrian' school and was one of those primarily responsible for bring-ing its message to America, to which he emigrated in 1940. At one level the book is a moving testimony to his struggle against the disasters which befell central Europe in the first half of the twentieth century. It is intended as a warning against the consequences of 'inflationism', 'interventionism', and 'socialism-communism', all of which, however, seem to be on a roughly equal footing as economic evils to be avoided. These are the tendencies which Mises blames for the dire fate of Austria at his time of writing (around 1940). It is therefore important to understand what these economic heresies actually entail. The latter two are fairly precisely defined in the text and do mean more or less what one would expect. Interventionism refers to an economic system which is nominally based on private ownership, but in which the government nonetheless attempts to exert a substantial degree of control via a series of regulations and decrees. These would include labour legislation, tariffs, wage and price regulation, environmental and safety stand-ards, and so on. Socialism-communism, meanwhile, refers to a system based on the public ownership of the means of production, in which the government controls every aspect of economic life. In contrast to these two, however, inflationism is nowhere so precisely defined.

There was, of course, a serious inflation in Austria in the aftermath of World War I, and a still more spectacular hyperinflation in Germany in 1922/23. If opposition to inflationism meant simply avoiding policies which would lead to these outcomes, then presumably there would be few who would disagree. However, it quickly becomes apparent that inflationism is implicitly defined much more broadly than that, and refers to any policy at all which might conceivably reduce either the internal or external value of the currency by even a small degree. For example, an anti-inflationist would certainly be a whole-hearted supporter of the gold standard, would balance the government budget at all times, and would oppose any attempt at a cheap money (low interest rate) policy. According to Mises any devaluation of the currency should be resisted, even by as little as 10 per cent (1978: 53). The possibility that these types of policies are the opposite of what a healthy capitalist economy would require, and that adherence to them would actually make interventionism and/or socialism-communism seem that much more attractive by comparison, is not considered. In Germany in the 1930s, as mentioned, Hitler was actually welcomed by many as a relief from Bruning and deflationism.

Even some fellow advocates of the market economy, such as Milton Friedman, have been critical of this fatalistic aspect of Austrian thought. Friedman (1974: 162–3), for example, noting that the London School of Economics (LSE) was a bastion of Austrian thought in the 1930s (through the influence of Lionel Robbins and Friedrich von Hayek) has written as follows:

> at the London School of Economics…the dominant view was that the depression was an inevitable result of the prior boom, that it was deepened by the attempts to prevent prices and wages from falling and firms from going bankrupt, that the monetary authorities had brought on the depression by inflationary policies before the crash and had prolonged it by 'easy money' policies thereafter; that the only sound policy was to let the depression run its course, bring down money costs, and eliminate weak and unsound firms.
>
> By contrast with this dismal picture, the news seeping out of Cambridge (England) about Keynes's interpretation of the depression and the right policy to cure it must have come like a flash of light on a dark night. It offered a far less hopeless diagnosis of the disease…It is easy to see how…young, vigorous, and generous mind(s) would have been attracted to it. …The intellectual climate at Chicago had been wholly different. My teachers regarded the depression as largely the product of misguided governmental policy – or at least as greatly intensified by such policies. They blamed the monetary and fiscal authorities for permitting banks to fail and the quantity of deposits to decline. Far from preaching the need to let deflation and bankruptcy run their course, they issued repeated pronunciamentos calling for government action to stem the deflation…
>
> …There was nothing in these views to repel a student; or to make Keynes attractive. On the contrary, so far as policy was concerned, Keynes had nothing to offer those of us who had sat at the feet of Simons, Mints, Knight, and Viner.

THE FREE-MARKET REVIVAL

Contrary to Schumpeter's predictions, it has turned out that advocates of free markets, including Mises and his US students (Sennholz, 1978), Hayek (1944, 1989) the leading 'Austrian' of the next generation, and Friedman himself (Friedman and Friedman, 1962, 1980), ultimately have had a great deal of influence on the political thought of the late twentieth century. Quite apart from the total disillusionment with, and rejection of, 'socialism-communism' in most of those countries where such regimes had been imposed, there was also a reaction against 'interventionism' in many of the non-socialist countries. As early as the late 1970s and early 1980s, elections had been won and governments were in power on platforms which explicitly promised to revitalize the role of the market in economic life. Most notable were the administrations of Margaret Thatcher in Britain and Ronald Reagan in the USA. As far as possible, market forces would be allowed to determine outcomes in the individual sectors of the economy. The influence of government, either via direct control, as in the nationalized industries, or via regulation and legislation, was to be reduced. In the much-used phrase of the period, the purpose was to 'roll back the frontiers of the state'. The conservative view was that this would not only lead to much greater prosperity due to the efficiency of the market mechanism, but also to greater political freedom by reducing state control over an important area of life.

In practice, and with different emphasis in different jurisdictions, the attempt to strengthen the role of market forces in economic life has taken four main routes. These are privatization (that is the sale of formerly state-owned industries to the private sector), deregulation, changes in labour and trade union legislation, and a reduction in the scope of the so-called 'welfare state'. Needless to say, there have been perennial complaints from free-market enthusiasts that the rhetoric of restoring market forces has not been matched by the reality in many cases, but it would be difficult to argue that there has not been a substantial change, in the political and intellectual climate around economic issues, from that described by Schumpeter.

One reason for the revival of interest in the market mechanism by the late twentieth century has been simply the result of several decades of experience of some of the alternatives, ranging from the centrally planned economies of the former USSR and its satellites to the operations of nationalized industries, marketing boards, and regulatory agencies in the industrialized democracies. This has provided a somewhat different perspective than had been available at the time of the publication of Schumpeter's book. By the time of Gorbachev's *perestroika* and *glasnost* (Gorbachev, 1988) in the mid-1980s, there could be little or no comparison between the moribund economies and miserable living conditions of the socialist countries and the relative prosperity of the West. This was so, even though, as described, conditions in the latter were hardly as favourable as they had once been. Arguably, it was economic breakdown, as much as the eventual rejection of totalitarianism, which ultimately led to the collapse of communism. Smithin (1982), drawing on the earlier work of Djilas (1957), argued that, ironically, the Marxian theory of historical materialism could actually be profitably applied to the case of the former Soviet bloc. Totalitarian communism, so far from representing either the endpoint of the historical process or a transitional stage on the road to some purer form of socialism, should actually be treated as simply another 'mode of production' in the Marxian sense. In the beginning, the class relationships characteristic of that mode of production, in particular the power of the party élites and the 'nomenklatura', and the ever-present element of coercion, were consistent with the type of economic development that was required (forced industrialization), however repugnant they may have been in terms of human rights. By the early 1980s, however, according to Smithin (1982: 55) it was clear that the political structure was now actually preventing further economic development, and, it was already possible, however tentatively, to see the signs of the eventual 'era of social revolution' (Marx, 1859; 1970: 21) which did in fact occur.

FLAWS IN THE ARGUMENT?

Granted, however, that the various forms of the totalitarian reaction to capitalism, including Mises's socialism-communism, and the earlier twentieth-century manifestations of National Socialism and Fascism, had lead to disaster, there is surely still a very serious question as to whether the appropriate response is to attempt to return to some mythical nineteenth-century *laissez-faire* capitalism. After all, it was experience with this system, and its ultimate denouement in World War I and the Depression, which is presumably what led to the communist/fascist reaction in the first place.

As mentioned in chapter 2, Milton and Rose Friedman, as leading advocates of *laissez-faire* in *Free to Choose* (1980), refer to the nineteenth century in both Britain and North America, when government intervention and regulation of the economy was much less, as a 'golden age'. The implication is that simply to turn the clock back, to undo most of the economic and social legislation of the twentieth century, would restore these ideal conditions. It was suggested earlier that what is strange about this argument is that although the nineteenth century was certainly an age of economic progress in some sense, the notion of it as a golden age is very much at variance with what we learn from social historians, and the social commentators, pamphleteers and novelists of the day. Simple proof that the extremes of *laissez-faire* were regarded with less than the Friedmans' enthusiasm by the populations which experienced them is that the pre-existing 'ideal' situation (from the Friedmans' point of view) can only have been transformed into the later 'unsatisfactory' one by a concrete historical process. The seeds of the uncompetitive state-regulated environment that conservative economists were bemoaning in the twentieth century must have been sown in that same past era in which private enterprise was supposedly flourishing. Quite obviously, the nineteenth century was *not* regarded as a golden age by many of those who had to live through it, and it was precisely the social and technical pressures arising out of nineteenth-century conditions which led ultimately to the growth of corporations, unions, minimum wage laws, administered prices, state ownership of industry, and the welfare state. According to Mises (1978: 13):

> By 1900 practically everyone in the German-speaking countries was either a statist [interventionist] or a state socialist. Capitalism was seen as a bad episode which fortunately had ended forever.

The obvious question to ask in response to this is, why? It is surely not reasonable to suggest that everything can be explained by simple perversity, stupidity, or propaganda. Similarly, during the Depression years, almost any other plausible alternative to the existing system would have seemed attractive. Galbraith (1994: 84), for example, commenting on the 'small, if vocal' communist element in the New Deal bureaucracy in the USA in the 1930s, suggests that:

> (h)ad such [communist] views not been present among those descending on Washington it would have been surprising. No one of any sensitivity could look on capitalism in those years and think it a success.

Hence, even if it was feasible to imagine that nineteenth-century conditions could be replicated in the present day, on past evidence one can only presume that this would be a temporary victory at best (Smithin, 1985). It must be assumed that the historical ball would soon start rolling once again. In other words, starting from a renewed *laissez-faire* environment, similar social pressures would emerge to push society back down the road it has already travelled.

We can suggest a number of basic reasons, aside from the technical sources of market failure listed in the textbooks, as to why these social pressures seem inevitably to emerge, in spite of the clear relative success of the market system in 'delivering the goods' (Robinson, 1964: 130) in aggregate.

First, even if everyone were to agree that a competitive market system provides the best economic environment for society as a whole, it is an obvious point that no individual, business firm or labour union has a *private* incentive to uphold market principles in their own sector of the economy. A business firm would prefer to be a monopolist in its particular product or products, union or professional association members would prefer a 'closed shop', and so on. Hence, *every* participant in the market economy is trying to escape from the conditions of the marketplace in their own field, and a large part of actual economic history is the record of that struggle. Paradoxically, therefore, state intervention (in the sense of the provision of a legal framework and competition policy, etc.) may be required simply to enable the market system itself to survive.

Second, a market system is a *competitive* system not only in the economist's technical sense but also (and more importantly) in the everyday sense of this term. There will be winners and losers, and this must be so if the system is to provide the incentives which are its life-blood. Those who have lost in the marketplace, however, have no incentive to stick to the rules of the game after the fact. On the contrary, they have a definite interest in attempting to reverse the market's verdict via the political process. To take just one example, it may be agreed that free trade will maximize welfare for a nation as a whole and for the world as a whole. For participants in an industry which will lose out to foreign competition, however, it will still be in their interests to resist free trade and advocate protectionism via the political process. The country as a whole may be worse off, and the world as a whole may be worse off, but the industry participants will be better off. Economic theory has suggested that if there are gains in aggregate, then the so-called 'compensation principle' should apply. It should be theoretically possible for the winners to somehow compensate the losers so that everyone is better off and will agree to the change. This is unlikely to be persuasive in practice, however, unless some mechanism can be found by which the compensation actually will be paid. This is a simple point which nonetheless seems to escape many welfare economists and cost-benefit analysts.

This is a general principle. In other areas beside trade, there will surely always have to be some kind of social contract, and presumably therefore a role for the state, to the effect that income should be redistributed, at least to some extent, such that those who do not do well out of the market process are more or less content to accept its verdict. This is not even a question of altruism or social justice. If the minimally necessary adjustments are not made, those who have 'lost' will simply have an incentive to undermine or overthrow the system via political means.

Third, even if individuals do well out of a market mechanism in terms of income, its results may not be acceptable on other grounds – moral, aesthetic or religious. The current revival of interest in environmental issues is a relatively straightforward example of this. Even on the simplest level, it may be true that market forces dictate that the countryside around major cities be swallowed up by ugly urban and suburban sprawl, but no amount of economic theory can force anyone to like it.[1]

For all of these reasons, it is unlikely that the free-market rhetoric and policies of the 1980s and 1990s will represent the last word in the continuing debate over the merits of the market mechanism. However, they have certainly changed the parameters of that debate from where they stood in the 1960s or 1970s. Nowadays, even opponents of out and out free market economics would tend to advocate not socialism but the so-called 'social market'. The supporters of this concept recognize the power of market forces for promoting prosperity, and hence would agree economic activity should take place in the market sector as far as possible. However, they would still leave a role for the state to diffuse some of the social pressures identified above by a certain amount of redistribution of incomes generated by the market process and legislation regarding codes of conduct in economic life.

MACROECONOMICS VERSUS MICROECONOMICS

In the policymaking tradition which developed in the immediate post-World War II period, it would have been argued that another of the sources of social pressure arising from a pure market system, which is more directly relevant to the subject of this volume, would be the lack of any mechanism in that system to ensure macroeconomic stability. One of the main themes of the return to classical or conservative economic thinking in more recent years, however, was a decisive rejection of this view. A pervasive argument of the influential new classical school,[2] for example, is that logically there should be no distinction between microeconomics and macroeconomics (Lucas, 1987). In the policy sphere, this translates into a general attitude that if *laissez-faire* or non-intervention is the best advice at the microeconomic level, this should apply at the level of the macroeconomy also. The authorities should simply withdraw from any attempt to stabilize the macroeconomy, and if they do so, the 'invisible hand' will ensure as desirable a macroeconomic outcome as at the level of an individual firm or industry. Somewhat inconsistently, it is widely agreed that the one exception to this rule is in the area of currency and prices. In this case, the central bank or government authorities should pursue very definite and rigid objectives, either zero inflation, a money supply rule, a fixed exchange rate, or membership of a currency union. One or other of these would be seen as necessary for price stability, which in turn would be held out as a prerequisite for the effective operation of the market mechanism. The only exceptions to this charge of inconsistency would be members of the neo-Austrian 'free banking' school, who would abolish state central banks entirely and believe that the unaided market mechanism itself would ensure practical price stability (Selgin and White, 1994).[3]

It might have been thought that the macroeconomic events of more recent years, discussed in the previous chapter, would have done something to shake the now mainstream view that there should be *laissez-faire* except for efforts to restore price stability. The environment has been anything but stable, with many of the disruptions evidently *caused* by adherence to the rigid conservative policy rules or formulas, supposedly designed to limit disruptive changes, in situations where the earlier policymaking tradition would have urged pragmatism and compromise. In the sense that these disruptions were caused explicitly by government action, it might still be possible to argue that the experience of the 1980s and 1990s provides yet another argument for the government to withdraw entirely from the economy, but at the end of the day this is a practical impossibility given the social pressures outlined above. It would therefore seem that with the continuing sheer size of governments in the real world,[4] they will have no option but to relearn the basic principles of macroeconomic management, at least in the negative sense of learning how not to rock the boat.

THE CONTRIBUTION OF KEYNES

Keynes was the one major economic thinker who did attempt, in his day, to articulate a 'middle way' (Skidelsky, 1992) between the extremes of the 'sterile left-right debate' in the economic sphere. Keynes's putative revolution was, of course, ultimately a failure, both in the attempt to change mainstream economic theory, which by now has reverted almost entirely to non-Keynesian or pre-Keynesian positions, and increasingly in the attempt to influence public attitudes in policy debates. Indeed, very few economists today would argue that there are any ready-made formulas from the 1930s or 1940s which can be removed from the shelf, dusted off, and applied without modification to contemporary problems. Nonetheless, Hamouda and Smithin (1988: x–xi) argue that Keynes's great contribution to the history of ideas was not in any particular theoretical construct or policy proposal, but simply in the notion that economic policy problems may be amenable to rational thought and management. They argue that before Keynes, and in many quarters after him, *both* the defenders of the economic system and its critics – the political forces of the right and the left – have taken what can only be described as an *alienated* view of macroeconomic problems. That is to say that the economy is seen as an external force which determines the fates of those who live under it but is not amenable to conscious control by them. For the believers in *laissez-faire* this is not disturbing, because the market economy, while sometimes harsh in its judgements on individuals, is ultimately benign from the point of view of society as a whole. It is a natural organism which only has to be left alone to provide the best of all possible worlds, in a material sense, for its grateful inhabitants. To the political left, the capitalist economy is equally an uncontrollable natural force, but in this case a demonic one, which only leads to misery and suffering for most of those in its power, and is proceeding via ever worsening crises to inevitable breakdown.

Keynes, who lived through World War I, Britain's economic stagnation and political crisis in the 1920s, and the worldwide Depression of the 1930s, was certainly not able to believe in *laissez-faire*, but was also not prepared to contemplate the collapse of the economic system and a totalitarian future, which would destroy the basis and values of civilization as he knew it. He came to believe that a third alternative was possible, that the system could be managed in order to retain the benefits and material standard of living that capitalism and the market system had made possible, and yet avoid its abuses. Not even the most ardent Keynesian could claim that Keynes fully spelled out the details of how this could be achieved in practice, and it is no doubt the case that Keynes's faith in government, as such, was influenced by his own secure position in the élite of British society, with its deeply ingrained paternalistic sense of public duty. It is also possible that observation of some of the actual attempts at economic management in the past 60 years would have made him more sceptical. None the less, the notion that society is not powerless in the face of the impersonal tides of the economy and history is Keynes's great contribution to the history of ideas.

In terms of reconciling a somewhat more activist approach to macroeconomic policymaking with the view that market systems are none the less more prosperous than the alternatives, it is worth recalling that when macroeconomic issues first came to dominate public discussion in the 1930s, Keynes himself saw no contradiction between these two points of view. Keynes, clearly, saw the major defects of the system as being macroeconomic rather than microeconomic in nature, with the main problem in his view being the lack of any automatic market mechanism to offset the impact of pervasive uncertainty about the future. In the absence of such a mechanism, there was no guarantee that the level of investment generated by a free enterprise system would always be adequate to maintain either full employment or long-run growth. Hence the need for the 'socialization of investment'.

This policy itself was vaguely defined and is subject to criticism on many grounds, but at the most it referred only to the minimum level of state intervention to ensure an adequate volume of total investment (public or private), and was very far short of outright nationalization or state control of the day-to-day operations of industry. The slogan also falls far short even of a complete description of macroeconomic policy, leaving open both the role of short-term 'fine tuning' policies and, crucially, the part to be played by monetary policy.[5] For present purposes however, the point is simply to stress Keynes's view that once the macroeconomics of the system were soundly managed the optimal microeconomic policy was to allow market forces to operate much as before. The issue is sufficiently important to justify the following lengthy quotation from the last chapter of *The General Theory* (1936: 377–81) itself:

> In some...respects the foregoing theory is moderately conservative...For whilst it indicates the vital importance of establishing certain central controls in matters which are now left in the main to individual initiative, there are wide fields of activity...unaffected...I conceive...that a somewhat comprehensive socialisation of investment will prove the only means of securing an approximation to full employment; though this need not exclude all manner of...devices by which public authority will cooperate with private initiative... beyond this no obvious case is made out for a system of State Socialism...
>
> ...(I)f our central controls succeed in establishing...full employment as nearly as is practicable...then there is no objection to be raised against the classical analysis of the manner in which private self-interest will determine what...is produced, in what proportions the factors of production will be combined to produce it, and how the value of the final product will be distributed between them...if we have dealt otherwise with the problem of thrift, there is no objection to be raised against the modern classical theory as to the degree of consilience between private and public advantage in conditions of perfect and imperfect competition respectively...apart from...the central controls there is no more reason to socialise economic life than there was before...
>
> ...Filling in the gaps in the classical theory is not to dispose of the 'Manchester System', but...indicate[s] the nature of the environment which the free play of economic forces requires...The central controls necessary to ensure full employment will...involve a large extension of the traditional functions of government. ...the modern classical theory has itself called attention to various conditions in which the free play of economic forces may need to be curbed or guided. But there will still remain a wide field for...private initiative and responsibility. Within this field the traditional advantages of individualism will still hold good...
>
> ...The authoritarian state systems of to-day seem to solve the problem of unemployment at the expense of efficiency and of freedom...(b)ut it may be possible by a right analysis of the problem to cure the disease whilst preserving efficiency and freedom.

Although this statement seems clear enough, Keynes's suggested resolution of the problem was (perhaps predictably) unpopular at both ends of the political spectrum. Conservatives would see the central controls in the macroeconomic sphere as simply the thin end of the wedge, whereas those to the left of centre who would be prepared to accept the macroeconomic analysis would also believe that Keynes should have gone much further in his critique of the market system (Robinson, 1964: 75–6, 81–2). Hence, in the years since

1936, both the opponents of Keynes and his ostensible defenders have tended to downplay his views on the market mechanism and economic efficiency at the microeconomic level.

In practice, also, it is evident that the clear separation of the macroeconomic and microeconomic problems as advocated by Keynes was not a feature of the so-called mixed economies of the western democracies in the post-World War II era. As discussed in chapter 2, macroeconomic policies were implemented which, if not precisely Keynesian, were at least inspired by Keynes, but at the same time many other economic changes, redolent of Mises's interventionism and socialism were occurring simultaneously. Hence, 'Keynesian' macroeconomics became inextricably associated in the public mind with a host of other policies which increased government intervention and state control of the economy at the microeconomic level. These would include the nationalization and regulation of industry, wage and price controls, capital controls,[6] rent controls, the growth of the welfare state, social insurance, redistributive taxation, agricultural price support schemes and marketing boards. In the popular imagination, therefore, by the end of the 1970s the expression Keynesianism had become little more than a code word for the general rise of government intervention and regulation of the economy.

CONCLUSION

The collapse of Soviet-style communism in the late 1980s and early 1990s has seemed to many finally to end the debate over the merits of the market economy or capitalism. This particular form of organization now seemed to be the 'only game in town'. However, on closer reflection, the situation is much less clear-cut than this immediate reaction would suggest. What the post-1989 events have actually done is simply to put an end to *one form* of the totalitarian reaction to capitalism and liberal democracy, much as did the outcome of World War II for the National Socialist and Fascist manifestations. What they have not done, ultimately, is to deal with or address the potential economic problems and difficulties which made the illiberal reaction seem plausible in the first place. Deflationism, falling prices, overvalued exchange rates, the obsession with balanced budgets, and orthodox finance in general, led to disaster in the 1930s. The partial liberation from these attitudes in the immediate postwar years, on the other hand, played a large part in the revival of the 'mixed economy' version of capitalism in the 1950s and 1960s.

A return to the canons of orthodox finance, which in essence means policies favouring the financial or rentier interests at the expense of both labour and non-financial business, has seemed to many enthusiasts of the market economy to be simply a natural corollary of the general revival of belief in the power of market forces and the benign effects of a return to *laissez-faire*. In this they seem to mistake the essential nature of the capitalist system, which does rely in a fundamental manner on the availability of financial credit at reasonable rates and on a spirit of optimism and expansiveness (Keynes's 'animal spirits'). These are stifled whenever the financial screws are excessively tight. As in the 1930s, there is a clear danger that the present obsession with policies of zero inflation and improving the rate of return to bondholders, with the commensurate disregard for economic opportunities and security for the average citizen that this implies, will ultimately lead to opposite economic and political results than those desired by their advocates.

NOTES

1. Having made this point, however, it is only fair to point out that whatever the environmental degradation caused by the capitalist economic process, the record of the so-called socialist states was far worse.
2. See chapter 3 below for a more complete discussion of the position of this school.
3. See Smithin (1994a) for further discussion and a critique.
4. For realistic appraisals, see Stein (1989: 6) and Johnson (1989: 1–14).
5. For further discussion of this concept, see Smithin (1989).
6. Both of the latter policies, admittedly, were frequently advocated by economists who would describe themselves as Keynesians, and in conjunction with more traditional Keynesian policy.

4. The power of ideas

INTRODUCTION

In *The General Theory* (1936: 383–4), Keynes made the following famous statement about the role of intellectual trends on the economic ideas of those in a position to make policy:

> the ideas of economists and political philosophers, both when they are right and when they are wrong, are more powerful than is commonly understood. Indeed the world is ruled by little else. Practical men, who believe themselves to be quite from any intellectual influences, are usually the slaves of some defunct economist. Madmen in authority…are distilling their frenzy from some academic scribbler of a few years back…soon or late, it is ideas, not vested interests, which are dangerous for good or evil.

This no doubt vastly underestimates the reciprocal influence of vested interests themselves on ideas, but it nonetheless contains a large element of truth, both for Keynes's time and our own. In particular, it is remarkable how certain economic ideas, on budget deficits, inflation, the global economy, etc., become accepted as 'facts' simply due to constant repetition in the print and electronic media. Yet a large proportion of the economic 'truths' or 'realities' which are so confidently paraded in the public arena basically just reflect the theoretical views of the currently dominant academic school. There is a pernicious side to this in that dissenting opinion at any point in time is frequently presented not just as a contribution to the debate, but as simple eccentricity flying in the face of the presumed scientific consensus. Arguments are prefaced by comments such as 'No sensible policymaker questions the view that…'[1] and, as in one memorable phrase from a recent Canadian newspaper, those who don't hold the consensus view at any point in time are dismissed as 'marginal crackpots'.[2]

It is true that many academic economists would like to claim for their subject something of the scientific precision which they perceive in the natural sciences. The motivation for this, however, seems to be nothing more exalted than a desire to attract some of the academic prestige and kudos which have traditionally been reserved for natural scientists. In other words, a sort of 'physics envy' as Mirowski (1989: 354) has aptly put it. To see what Mirowski means, consider, for example, the description by the Nobel prizewinner, Paul Samuelson (1983), of his own youthful *magnum opus, Foundations of Economic Analysis* (1947; 1983). The words 'science', 'scientist' and 'scientific' are used repeatedly, and the author manages to get in references to Newton, Euler, Maxwell, Poincare, Watson, Helmholz, Faraday, Einstein and Gibbs, among others, in an introduction to what is ostensibly, after all, a book on economics.[3] This may be an extreme example, but more generally it would be impossible to deny that this spirit of 'scientism' in modern economics has led to an increasing and overwhelming formalization and mathematization of the academic literature. It can be argued that this has come at the expense of any advance in the understanding of the economy *per se*. As illustrated by the work of historians of thought such as Humphrey (1993), essentially the same debates are recycled in each generation, but at increasingly complex levels of mathematical sophistication.

A more attractive and relevant model for economics is provided by Hicks (1983: 365) who considers the subject to be a 'discipline not a science', and who quotes approvingly Keynes's dictum from the preface to the old *Cambridge Economics Handbooks* series:

> The Theory of Economics does not furnish a body of settled conclusions immediately applicable to policy. It is a method rather than a doctrine, a technique of thinking, which helps its possessor to draw correct conclusions.[4]

In any event the purpose of this chapter is to examine the seemingly endless twists and turns of the 'conventional wisdom' on macroeconomic issues, and, in turn, to enquire what effect these changes have had on actual economic outcomes. What are the political, intellectual and economic forces which lie behind these apparently contradictory changes in the climate of opinion?

CHANGING FASHIONS IN MACROECONOMIC THOUGHT

Aside from Marxism, which was obviously the decisive force in many parts of the globe before 1989, there seem to have been three main intellectual 'waves' which have influenced macroeconomic policymaking in the non-socialist world during the twentieth century.

First, prior to the Great Depression of the 1930s, and the publication of Keynes's *The General Theory of Employment Interest and Money* (1936), thinking on macroeconomic problems was dominated by the views of what Keynes called the 'classical' school.[5] This was essentially a doctrine of *laissez-faire*, in which it was believed that governments could do little and should do little about macroeconomic performance, except in the area of currency and prices.

In contrast, in the second phase, during the 25 years or so after World War II down to the break-up of the Bretton Woods system in 1971–73 the dominating viewpoint was radically different. This period is frequently described (rightly or wrongly) as the heyday of 'Keynesian' economics, during which it was widely believed that government fiscal and monetary policies do have important economic effects. Consequently, it was now thought that one of the main responsibilities of democratic government was to ensure the smooth operation of the economy. There is serious doubt, however, as to how closely the consensus view of the day actually corresponded to the work of Keynes himself, as will be discussed below.

The third wave of fashionable thinking about the economy was then the so-called 'conservative revolution' beginning in the late 1970s and early 1980s. This, in many ways, simply represented a swing of the pendulum back to points of view which were in vogue before the 1930s. Hence the epithet 'new classical' as applied to one set of academic theories which have supported the conservative view.

Having identified these major swings of opinion, the drawbacks of relying on the consensus view of the day are apparent. In essence, the views are highly time dependent. The consensus opinion today may be the opposite of what it was 20 or 30 ago, and may well be something else again 20 years hence.

EMPIRICAL PROBLEMS IN MACROECONOMICS

In the realm of academic economics, the official method of confronting economic theories with facts, and hence forming some kind of conclusion on the merits of the competing approaches, is via econometrics; the application of statistical methods to economic data. However, in spite of the impressive level of technical sophistication in much contemporary econometric work, econometric testing *per se* has rarely been decisive in settling economic controversies (Summers, 1991; Smithin, 1995b). There is a large gap between professed views on the appropriate methods of testing competing theories and the actual practice of theory appraisal, with the latter highly dependent on subjective, sociological and environmental factors (Pheby, 1988; Dow, 1988). Also, increasingly, the conceptual foundations of econometrics, and of statistical induction in general, are once again the subject of methodological debate (Pheby, 1988).

The relative lack of success of econometric testing in discriminating between alternative theories, however, does not mean that there is no relation-

ship between economic theory and the facts. What seems to have been decisive in practice is whether or not the theory corresponds with the basic 'facts
of experience', on such things as unemployment or inflation, which are more
or less readily apparent in everyday life. A particular threat to an entrenched
theory arises when an empirical problem becomes 'anomalous', that is to say
when one particular theory cannot explain the current situation but another,
competitor, theory seemingly can (Laudan, 1977).

An obvious example of an empirical problem for an economic theory was
the impact of the mass unemployment of the 1930s on the status of the
macroeconomics of the classical school. The position of that school ruled out
so-called 'involuntary unemployment', and it was believed that any actual
deviations of unemployment rates from full employment would be short-
lived and quickly corrected by market forces. Evidently, the experience of the
Great Depression of the 1930s would provide a particularly awkward empirical difficulty for economists who accepted this view. This would then go
some way towards explaining the shift in the consensus opinion after World
War II. Nonetheless, even such a glaring discrepancy was only a potential
problem until a rival theory emerged, which was able to explain the empirical
problem by the subjectively determined academic standards of the day. In the
1930s, the *apparently* successful competitor theory was that of Keynes.

'ORTHODOX' KEYNESIANISM

With the hindsight of more than half a century, however, it is obviously
highly debatable whether Keynes's work was ultimately successful in estab-
lishing an alternative research tradition among economists, either at the academic or policymaking level. Among so-called 'Post Keynesian' economists
(Davidson, 1991, 1994; Lavoie, 1992a), a group who claim a more faithful
adherence to the original writings of Keynes than the mainstream of the
economics profession, the standard view is that the Keynesian revolution
never really came to fruition, and that the orthodoxy which emerged after
World War II was simply a variation on the general theme of mainstream
economics, owing little to Keynes himself. Because of this debate, it should
be stressed that in this chapter the consensus view which developed in the
postwar period will be referred to as 'orthodox' Keynesianism, following
Snowden *et al.* (1994: 89–123), as opposed to either Post Keynesianism or
the original work of Keynes.

Even if it did deviate from the original blueprint, however, initially the
orthodox version of Keynesian seemed to be successful enough on its own
terms. Its central principle was aggregate demand management, with the
objective of moderating fluctuations of output and employment around what

were variously described as their 'potential', or 'capacity', or 'full employment' levels.

In textbook Keynesian theory, aggregate demand management by the government might be achieved by either fiscal or monetary policy, but in practice during the Keynesian era in most jurisdictions the emphasis was very much on fiscal policy. This was consistent with the fact that policy was being carried on against the backdrop of the Bretton Woods system of fixed exchange rates, implying that world monetary policy was essentially determined by the actions of the US Fed. In this context, if a national economy was in recession, for example, with output below its potential level, and unemployment high, this would be attributed to a lack of aggregate demand for goods and services. The remedy (to the dismay of fiscal conservatives) would be either for the government simply to add directly to aggregate demand by increasing spending, or alternatively to cut taxes, thus leaving more purchasing power in the hands of the consumer. Conversely, if aggregate demand was too high and inflation was threatening, the idea (theoretically) would be that the authorities should cut spending or raise taxes.

An apparently obvious gap in this framework is that the emphasis on smoothing fluctuations around some arbitrarily defined norm may well deflect attention away from what might be regarded as the more pressing task of improving the potential output or average underlying growth rate of the economy. For decades, however, this omission seemed to require little attention, at either the theoretical or practical policy level, one reason being that the years of Keynesian demand management, whether coincidentally or not, were also years of healthy underlying average growth rates. In such circumstances, it must have seemed that the growth rate could take care of itself, and smoothing the business cycle could become the ultimate goal of policy.

THE COLLAPSE OF ORTHODOX KEYNESIANISM IN THE 1970s

Such was the position as it stood towards the end of the 1960s, but by the mid-1970s, orthodox Keynesianism was itself facing serious empirical problems, which its critics would regard as chickens finally coming home to roost, albeit after a long delay. These empirical problems played a large part in the (apparently temporary) joint triumph of both monetarism and the original 'monetary misperceptions' version of new classical theory. The latter theories, in turn, seemed to have a rather short-lived reign, and were hit with empirical problems of their own almost immediately, leading to the present unsettled situation on the theoretical front.

There were two empirical problems which faced orthodox Keynesianism in the 1970s, and were regarded as serious at the time. The first was simply the double-digit inflation which occurred in most of the industrialized nations. The second was the new phenomenon of stagflation.

The experience of inflation was a problem for Keynesian economics both because of the widespread view that Keynesian models were not well-equipped to deal with inflationary problems, and also a deep-seated suspicion that the application of Keynesian policies was itself actually causing the situation.

It is not strictly correct that the logic of textbook Keynesian theory cannot be adapted to inflationary problems. Within that framework, distinctions can be made (for example) between 'demand-pull' and 'cost-push' inflation. Hence various remedies for inflation, such as reductions in aggregate demand, and/ or wage and price controls to reduce cost pressures, can be suggested. None the less, for 30 or more years the emphasis on problems of capacity utilization, output and employment had been so pronounced that there was indeed a widespread perception that Keynesian economics would be less helpful in an inflationary environment. At the textbook level, for instance, authors typically went beyond the assumption that nominal wages are 'sticky' to assume that both nominal wages and nominal prices were absolutely fixed. This strategy, evidently, then made it difficult to sustain the theory as relevant and interesting when both wages and prices were demonstrably changing quite rapidly.

More substantively, it was also argued that the suggested Keynesian remedies for inflation are politically asymmetrical in the democracies. To take fiscal policy as an example, the remedy for a recession would be either increases in government spending or reductions in taxes, both of which are usually politically popular. To reduce inflationary pressures by fiscal means, however, would require either spending cuts or increases in taxes, which are less so. Hence the view that in the real world Keynesian policies are biased in an inflationary direction.

There were also alleged to be more direct channels by which Keynesian policies would cause inflation, through, for example, the encouragement of an irresponsible monetary policy via the 'monetization' of budget deficits. This latter view assumes that Keynesian fiscal policies do ultimately lead to an excess of government expenditure over taxation, and further that the deficit will be financed not by straightforward borrowing (bond sales to the public) but by selling the bonds to the government's own central bank which then creates the funds to pay for them simply by increasing the monetary base. In the former case, at least on monetarist principles, there would be no inflation because there is no increase in the money supply. In the latter, however, the increase in the monetary base leads to an increase in the overall money supply and inflation will ensue. Although it might seem that the decision to debt finance or money finance is therefore a clear-cut policy choice, by the late 1970s a number of economists had begun to argue that there really is no choice at all. Sooner or later, debt financing will become untenable and ultimately pressures to monetize and inflate will become irresistible (Sargent and Wallace, 1981). Obviously, later experience rather casts doubt on this view, at least for the industrialized countries (there are several examples of budget deficits rising dramatically as inflation rates fell), but the point here is simply that this type of argument was another influential factor in the demise of orthodox Keynesianism in the late 1970s.

THE RISE OF MONETARISM

The inflationary situation of the 1970s then, together with the difficulties that the orthodox Keynesian approach seemed to be facing in that context, provided an intellectual climate in which the theory of monetarism[6] became very attractive. Monetarism explicitly placed inflation at the centre of the stage, and had an extremely simple and understandable explanation of the phenomenon. This was simply that the long-run average inflation rate (over a period of years rather than months or quarters) was mainly determined by the underlying average rate of growth of the money supply. This was backed up by the apparently overwhelming statistical evidence of money–nominal income correlations stretching back over a long period of history in many countries (Friedman, 1983). Moreover, crucially, in the version provided by Friedman and Schwartz (1963) monetarism was not only able to solve the empirical problem presented to Keynesians by inflation, but was also able to provide an alternative explanation of the earlier phenomenon which had given rise to Keynesianism in the first place, the Great Depression.

In monetarist theory, even though in the long-run increases or decreases in the rate of monetary growth will affect only the inflation rate, and are neutral with respect to real output and employment, allowance is made for an interim period in which changes in monetary growth rates do cause temporary changes in real GDP growth rates and labour market outcomes. Thus, although a 'tight money' policy will ultimately bring down the inflation rate, the argument is that it will first push the economy into recession. Similarly, the first impact of an 'easy money' policy will be a temporary boom, and only later will the boom evaporate in inflation. In the case of the Great Depression, the large declines in output and employment could then be explained, within the monetarist framework, by a particularly perverse monetary policy on the part of the Federal Reserve System which allowed the narrowly defined money supply to fall by as much as one-third in the period 1929–33 (Friedman and Friedman, 1980: 70–90).[7] On the monetarist logic, then, it was possible to simultaneously blame the policy of the Federal Reserve for *both* the inflationary environment of the 1970s and the Great Depression, and yet also to deny the possibility of any permanent benefits in terms of output and employment from activist monetary management. This was a powerful combination of arguments in the political and economic circumstances of the 1970s.

THE NEW CLASSICAL SCHOOL

The other major empirical problem for orthodox Keynesianism in the 1970s, namely the occurrence of the stagflationary episodes in which both unemployment and the inflation rate were rising, also in a sense provided an opportunity for a competing economic theory to gain a foothold. In this case, however, the process was a little less direct.

Within the broadly Keynesian tradition it is, in fact, possible to argue that stagflation is the result of 'supply shocks', rather than changes in aggregate demand, in which case the association of rising prices and falling output is fairly readily explained. Furthermore, as far as the 1970s is concerned, the two OPEC oil crises obviously present themselves as possible candidates for the source of such shocks. If this line of argument became clear to both orthodox Keynesians and others after the event, however, it was less so at the time. Whatever the true cause of stagflation, its immediate impact on the economics profession was to cause a severe crisis of confidence within the orthodox macroeconomics of the day. It was this crisis of confidence, plausibly, which provided an opening for an even more formidable theoretical competitor than monetarism. This was the 'rational expectations with monetary misperceptions' version of the 'new classical' macroeconomics, as propagated by Lucas (1981) and others, which was able to achieve a commanding theoretical position in what seems in retrospect a very short period of time.

To the extent that orthodox Keynesian economics had become identified with the large-scale econometric models of the day, the empirical problem posed by stagflation was particularly severe (Lucas and Sargent, 1981). These models tended to have a demand side consisting of an extended IS/LM model, and a supply side consisting essentially of a Phillips-curve relationship with a *negative* trade-off between inflation and unemployment (hence, a positive relationship between inflation and output). So constrained, they clearly could not predict the opposite situation of stagflation, and inevitably the actual occurrence of stagflation was a major blow to the credibility of these models (Lucas, 1981: 283).

In terms of broad intellectual history, it is by no means clear why the name of Keynes should be so firmly associated with the later work of Phillips, and (even more incongruously) with econometric work in the direct line of descent from the pioneering efforts of Tinbergen which Keynes had so harshly criticized (Keynes, 1939). However, the large-scale econometric models had certainly come to be regarded as 'Keynesian' by the majority of the economics profession in the 1970s, and hence empirical problems for the econometricians were thereby empirical problems for Keynesianism also.

It cannot plausibly be claimed that new classical theory evolved specifically as a response to the empirical difficulties of Keynesian models during the 1970s, as some of the decisive contributions were published (and certainly must have been written) before the nature of these difficulties became fully evident. However, the apparent collapse of Keynesian econometrics was clearly a major factor in their rapid acceptance.

THE ROLE OF CONCEPTUAL PROBLEMS

Other factors were at work also, which no doubt seem more important to those inside the economics profession than those outside it, but whose importance should not be underestimated. In addition to empirical difficulties of the type discussed above, the fate and acceptability of any particular economic theory is also profoundly influenced by its ability to solve conceptual problems which arise in the development and articulation of the theory itself.

In economics, it is clear that the theoretical debate in the mainstream literature of the modern period has entirely revolved around *internal* conceptual problems (Laudan, 1977: 48–54; Pheby, 1988: 71–3), specifically the extent to which the competing theories can be reconciled with the preferred central axiom that economic agents are rational (self-interested) optimizers or maximizers. Contemporary mainstream economic theory is notable for the extreme tenacity with which it adheres to this principle, and in some quarters this has hardened into the view that there can be no valid economic theory which is not consistent with it. For macroeconomics, this means that behaviourial functions of macroeconomic models are considered suspect unless it can be demonstrated that they are consistent with rational optimizing behaviour at the microeconomic level, with firms maximizing profits, consumers maximizing utility and so on. This is the point of the vast literature on the microeconomic 'underpinnings' of macroeconomics.

The non-economist might well be prepared to dismiss the methodological preferences of economists as just so much arid scholasticism, but, in fact, the tendency of economists to appraise competing theories in this way does have important repercussions both for the tone of the policy debate and for the actual conduct of policy itself. In particular, Keynesian economics, broadly defined, has always had difficulties on this score, and hence has always been on the defensive in terms of methodological purity.

The professed purpose of what was called the 'neoclassical synthesis' of the 1950s and 1960s was precisely to reconcile Keynesian macroeconomic ideas with standard microeconomics, but it quickly became apparent that the mainstream Keynesian economics of that era could only 'work' (in the sense of providing a theoretical explanation for the observation that fluctuations in *nominal* aggregate demand could have real effects on the economy) by abandoning the cherished first principle of rational optimizing agents in certain key areas. Early IS/LM-type expositions, for example, rested on the assumption that nominal wages were rigid or at least 'sticky' (Hicks, 1937; Modigliani, 1944). Later, during the Phillips-curve era, the non-neutrality of fiscal and monetary policy in Keynesian models depended on more complicated disequilibrium wage and price dynamics whose existence rested on the assumption of 'adaptive expectations', a rule of thumb that expectations of future economic variables (such as the price level) would be based on some simple extrapolation of a weighted average of past observations of those variables.[8]

The point is that in neither case was the crucial assumption, wage rigidity or adaptive expectations, based on a convincing micro-theoretical argument as to why rational optimizing agents would set wages or form expectations in this way. Hence, key elements of the model would always be vulnerable to attack by methodological purists. It goes without saying that in arguments of this kind, observations that in practice nominal wages *do* tend to be sticky are no defence. There must also be some explanation of *why* wages tend to be sticky which is consistent with the basic methodological presupposition of rational maximizing agents.

This last statement, however, probably overstates the element of anti-empiricism that is involved. The interaction between empirical and conceptual problems in economics is actually more subtle than this. It would be more accurate to say that during the heyday of the orthodox Keynesian era, Keynesian macroeconomic models were accepted on sufferance by methodological purists in the economics profession. They were marginally acceptable (a) because they seemed to work in the sense of being broadly consistent with the facts, (b) because Keynesian macroeconomic policies based on those models also seemed to work, and (c) crucially, because there was nothing better. However, as soon as the empirical difficulties with Keynesian models became obvious in the 1970s, the patience of mainstream theorists with Keynesianism quickly wore thin, and there were very few who were inclined to defend it.

Hence, the ideas of Lucas and his colleagues in the 1970s fell on fertile ground. Mainstream economists had long been unhappy with the underpinnings of the conventional Keynesian-type models which were presented to them, but could do little about this as long as they were empirically successful and there was nothing else on the horizon. It was this awkward situation, however, which set the stage for the rapid rise of the new classical school in the 1970s. The empirical failures of the orthodox Keynesian models at the time meant that the approach could now be dispensed with by a profession which had become increasingly sceptical. Then, what Lucas and the other new classicals were also able to do was to provide an alternative explanation of macroeconomic phenomena which was much more firmly based on the preferred methodology. At the time, the Lucas theory seemed able to solve the empirical problems of *both* the original classical school of the 1930s, and those of the orthodox Keynesians of the 1970s, in a way which satisfied the desire of academic economists to bring the awkward and untidy discipline of macroeconomics safely back within the fold of standard economic theory.

It also satisfied a potentially more important set of constituents, and here the interface between vested interests and ideas is more clearly visible. From the political and ideological point of view, the theory was able to explain the broad features of the business cycle in a way which did not allow for any corrective action on the part of government. At best, a systematic activist government would be impotent, and at worst an unsystematic policy would actually contribute to the cycle. The political conclusion which could be drawn was that governments should abandon any attempts to manage the macroeconomy, and interfere as little as possible. It was this implication, in particular, which caught the attention of those who might otherwise have dismissed the whole approach as just another example of the tendency of contemporary economists to retreat into the wasteland of abstract mathematical theory. The 'new classical' theory of the late 1970s and early 1980s, abstract though it may have been, was sending a message which was consistent with that of the most influential political forces of the day.

THE POLICY IRRELEVANCE PROPOSITION

In the Lucas–Sargent–Barro new classical framework, the distinction between the anticipated and unanticipated components of demand-side government policy was believed to be crucial. If government policy is correctly *anticipated* (i.e., policies are following some set pattern discernable from past behaviour, and do turn out as expected), rational economic agents should be able to work out the consequences for the behaviour of nominal magnitudes such as money wages or prices. They can then incorporate this knowledge into their plans of action (e.g. when negotiating labour contracts). If the response of the agents is not constrained in any way, for instance by existing nominal contracts still in force, then their actions should effectively offset the impact of the demand-side government policy and neutralize its effect on the real economic variables such as real wages, relative prices, output and employment.

If the policy changes are *unanticipated*, however, meaning either that the policy changes are random or that there is some change in direction which is not discernable from past behaviour or credible announcements, even rational economic agents may confuse the resulting change in nominal magnitudes with the changes in real prices that are relevant to them. This (rational) confusion or 'misperception' of real and nominal magnitudes will therefore cause economic agents to rationally but *mistakenly* change their levels of real economic activity.

The resulting theory is then consistent with statistical observation of Phillips-curve type correlations between real and nominal magnitudes, and the random or unpredictable element of government policy actually emerges as one of the various shocks which is driving the business cycle. This part of governmental policy should therefore (presumably) be eliminated. On the other hand, it is impossible to construct a systematic and intelligible policy which might itself do something to smooth the cycle,[9] as any systematic counter-cyclical policy can be understood and anticipated by the economic agents. Hence it will be impotent. This 'policy irrelevance' proposition was clearly the complete negation of the spirit of Keynesian activism which had guided policy before the 1970s.

The stagflationary episodes which had caused problems for the orthodox Keynesians could easily be accommodated within the general framework of new classical theory by postulating an increase in the pressure of aggregate demand which is confidently anticipated, but does not actually transpire. The agents will respond to the anticipated increase in demand by pushing up prices, hence the inflation, but will find when the time comes that there is insufficient aggregate demand to sustain sales at those prices, hence the falls in output and employment (Parkin, 1982: 412–14).

In terms of predicting economic outcomes the new classical model seemed to be able to do everything promised by the orthodox Keynesian model and more. Yet its central message was that the authorities would be best advised to abandon any attempt to manage the economy. According to the logic of the new classical economics, governments could not hope to do any good, and if they persisted in trying they would be more likely to do harm. Their actions would simply represent just one of many sources of random and unpredictable shocks with which the private sector has to contend.

THE NEW CLASSICAL SCHOOL AND MONETARISM

The relationship between the late 1970s/early 1980s version of new classical theory and the older doctrine of monetarism is interesting. At the time of the original conservative revolution both could claim to be gaining adherents at a rapid rate, although obviously it had taken the monetarists a lot longer to get into that position. The point seems to be that in its earliest incarnation at least, the new classical theory was seen as highly compatible with monetarism, both in its specific policy conclusions and its general ethos regarding the role of government in the economy (Hoover, 1984). Therefore, although the new classical theory was incomparably more sophisticated technically than monetarism, it may be said that the gradual rise of monetarist ideas was one of the forces paving the way for the eventual rapid acceptance of the first wave of the new classical theory. This is so even given the later disagreements between these two groups.

The new classical theory actually endorsed the central tenet of monetarism without reservation. In the new classical scheme, a fully anticipated change in rate of growth of the nominal money supply would immediately be reflected in a commensurate increase in the inflation rate, and over the long-run, the average inflation rate would be governed by the underlying rate of monetary growth. In this sense, the quantity theory of money remained intact.

Moreover, in the beginning it seemed that the new classical theory added a helpful twist to the monetarist case for an anti-inflation policy. The major political problem faced by monetarists trying to translate their theories into action in the circumstances of the late 1970s and early 1980s was that they had traditionally accepted the short-run non-neutrality of money. Hence, the major policy problem of the time, a transition from a high-inflation to a low-inflation environment, was seen as a much more difficult task than maintaining a low inflation rate to start with. Starting from the high-inflation situation, a tight money policy would first cause a recession in real economic activity, well before the benefits of lower inflation would be perceived. The tight money policy might be defended with slogans such as 'short-term pain for long-term gain' but there is always the possibility that electorates in democratic states might evaluate the benefit/cost ratio differently than the economists. What the new classical theory did, on this political front, was to hold out the promise that the awkward trade-off could be avoided. If the reduction in the rate of growth of the money supply was fully anticipated, there need be no short-run real effects and there could be 'disinflation without tears'. All that was required was that the proposed disinflation be announced in advance and be 'credible'. This was a message, of course, which was highly palatable to monetarist economists and politicians trying to persuade the public that a strong anti-inflation policy was necessary. Hence the new classical economists, by and large, tended originally to be accepted by the monetarists as their allies, even though many traditional monetarists later had second thoughts (Laidler, 1990).

WHICH TYPE OF KEYNESIANISM?

The scenario which has been set out so far is one in which macroeconomic policymaking in the immediate postwar years was dominated by orthodox Keynesianism, with an emphasis on short-run demand management, which was apparently highly successful for the first two postwar decades but then fell apart during the inflationary and stagflationary 1970s. The stage was then set for the rise of both monetarism and the new classical school, together comprising a new orthodoxy which would avoid any attempt to consciously manage the macroeconomy, except for control of the money supply to reduce inflation.

Although this may not be a bad broad brush description of the state of affairs in mainstream economics around 1979 or 1980, the picture can be and has been challenged on a number of grounds.

For dedicated free-marketeers, for example, the satisfactory economic performance of the industrialized economies after World War II must obviously be attributed not to government policy but solely to market forces, however unconvincing this may seem to be from a historical perspective. More interestingly, there have been doubts expressed on other grounds also. In the case of Britain, for example, Matthews (1968) doubted that the success in maintaining full employment down to his time of writing could be attributed to orthodox Keynesian demand management policy. This was on the grounds that the central government current budget had been in surplus throughout much of the relevant period. His explanation was that an investment boom had taken place, which may have been encouraged by government policy in some sense, but not necessarily by the orthodox demand management policies with which Keynesian economics had become identified.

This line of reasoning, in fact, would not be uncongenial to those economists of the Post Keynesian school who have argued that Keynesian economics should *not* be exclusively identified with the 'fine-tuning' demand management exercises of the textbooks. It has been pointed out, for example, that the main policy recommendation of Keynes's *General Theory* was not demand management *per se*, but the so-called 'socialization of investment' (1936: 378), which is properly interpreted not as the genuinely socialist policy of nationalization, but whatever action could be taken by the state to encourage more investment in both the public and private sectors. It has been stressed that in helping to formulate the plans for British postwar employment policy which are recorded in wartime Treasury memoranda, Keynes (1980b: 322) made it clear that the investment policy should be part of a 'stable long-term programme' and not a counter-cyclical fine-tuning strategy (Meltzer, 1998). On the view of the world that Keynes was apparently taking in these contributions, the potential flaw of market-orientated economic systems is not so much at the level of the microeconomic operation of the price system (1936: 379–81), but the lack of a reliable mechanism *in a world of uncertainty* to ensure that an adequate aggregate level of investment spending will always be forthcoming. The role of the state is then simply to do whatever it can to make sure that the flow of investment, public or private, continues (Smithin, 1989; Meltzer, 1988).

Some economists have recently argued that the relative economic success experienced in the industrialized countries after World War II may actually be due to the rudimentary application of this more 'fundamental' Keynesian policy rather than the traditional fine-tuning. Kregel (1985), for example, presents evidence that in several countries the direct state contribution to fixed capital formation increased after World War II, tending to peak in the early 1960s and declining thereafter. Pressman (1987) has also presented similar evidence for the USA alone. This line of research would indicate that the conventional idea of what 'Keynesian' policy actually is may require major revision.

This view is also consistent with the idea that Keynesian policy should be particularly identified with 'cheap money' or low interest rates. More specifically, though Keynes and many of the early Keynesian writers did not make much distinction between real and nominal interest rates, Smithin and Wolf (1993: 373) have argued that in contemporary conditions 'Keynesian' policies should generally be associated with attempts to bring about low real rates of interest on financial instruments. Although this point may not be stressed in the standard textbooks it can none the less be argued that this is the interpretation which is most consistent with Keynes's own writing. It is supported, for example, by Kaldor (1986: xxi) and at the other end of the professional spectrum by Meltzer (1988), in a book-length study. When Keynes himself was called on to defend the Bretton Woods agreement in 1944, against the charge that the new world financial arrangements would make expansionary policy in a single jurisdiction impossible, he replied as follows in a speech to the House of Lords (1980a: 16–19):

> (w)e are determined that, in future, the external value of sterling shall conform to its internal value as set by our own domestic policies and not the other way round...we intend to retain control of our domestic rate of interest, so that we can keep it as low as suits our own purposes...whilst we intend to prevent inflation at home, we will not accept deflation at the dictate of influences from outside...
>
> Have those responsible for the monetary arrangements been sufficiently careful to preserve these principles from the possibility of interference? I hope your Lordships will trust me not to have turned my back on all I have fought for.

It is by no means clear that Keynes's defence of Bretton Woods was convincing, but the point of the quotation is that it does clearly indicate his priorities regarding interest rates.

Certainly, Keynes seemed to hold different views at different times on whether monetary policy *per se* was adequate to lower interest rates and bring about full employment. In *The General Theory* he was sceptical, hence the alternative policy of the socialization of investment. This was also supposed to lead to the 'euthanasia of the rentier' (1936: 374) via some (not fully explained) process of capital saturation. In other places, as in the quotation above, the rate of interest seems to be simply an exogenous policy-determined variable. This is a point of view which has more recently been restated by some later Post Keynesians, such as Moore (1988), Kaldor (1986) and Lavoie (1992a). Either way, there is a clear implication that some of the policies that routinely are described as 'Keynesian' in the standard literature should really not be, because of their association with high real rates of interest rather than low rates. This would apply to many of the IS/LM or IS/LM/BP exercises of the textbooks, as discussed in more detail in chapter 6 below.

All of these points were apparently lost on the orthodox Keynesians of the 1950s and 1960s, and the alternative interpretation of Keynes had little or no influence on the climate of ideas when the crunch for Keynesianism came in the 1970s. The failure of the large-scale econometric models therefore meant that monetarist and new classical economists were able to seize their opportunity. By the late 1970s, the stage was set for what might be described as the first wave of the conservative revolution, the 'monetarist experiment' of 1979–82.

EMPIRICAL PROBLEMS FOR THE 'NEW' MACROECONOMIC THEORIES

It is ironic, however, that the actual course of events in the 1980s and 1990s has caused just as many empirical problems for both monetarist theory, and the original version of new classical theory, as had plagued the orthodox Keynesian school in the 1970s. The new theories had the misfortune to be put to the test almost as soon as they had acquired popularity, and in many respects were found wanting.

One of the earliest casualties was the policy irrelevance proposition of the new classical school. As described, the sharp distinction which this school had made between the anticipated and unanticipated components of macroeconomic policy simultaneously ruled out the possibility of any effective activist policy stance and also held out the promise of a painless disinflation if only the public understood the determination of the authorities to achieve this. The experience of the tight-money recessions of the early 1980s, and for that matter both the US fiscal policy-induced recovery of the mid-1980s and the later round of tight money recessions in 1990/91, has exploded this view. In all of these cases, the implications of the policy changes were widely discussed and understood and yet their impact (qualitatively) was more or less what an old-fashioned orthodox Keynesian economist would have pre-dicted. Such an economist equipped with only an old textbook, paying no attention to model consistency, rational expectations, or micro-underpinnings, who also kept up with the financial press, would have surely made a better job of predicting the course of events in the early to mid-1980s than his or her colleagues schooled in the latest 'high-tech' theory of the day (Tobin, 1986b: 351).

Not only did the early versions of new classical economics run into empiri-cal difficulties by the early 1980s, but so also did traditional monetarism. It has certainly been established that a tight-money policy can reduce inflation rates via high real interest rates, a tightening of credit conditions, and an enforced slowdown of economic activity. The preferred monetarist descrip-tion of this process, however, in terms of relationships between the growth rates of monetary aggregates and nominal incomes and inflation rates, broke down in the 1980s in what was also a period of rapid financial innovation. The classic example of this was in Britain when the Thatcher government chose sterling M3 as the monetary aggregate to watch in their anti-inflation-ary policy. As inflation came down (because, among other things, there really was a tight-money, high interest rate policy in place) the particular sterling M3 aggregate actually rose. This was just an extreme example of a general phenomenon, implying that the conduct of monetary policy in a rapidly changing environment should be a more pragmatic exercise than simply setting target growth rates for particular current definitions of the money supply.

The more extreme monetarist proposition that there is an iron link between government budget deficits and inflation, via the monetization of deficits, has also suffered a severe empirical blow. The fight against inflation was success-ful on its own terms in the 1980s and 1990s, but budget deficits rose to record levels. As suggested in chapter 6 below, cause and effect in these relation-ships may well be the opposite of what the notion of 'unpleasant monetarist arithmetic' would suggest.

Even the most central feature of mainstream macroeconomics, the idea that there is a 'natural' rate of unemployment towards which the economy inevitably gravitates, has run into difficulties in the renewed era of mass unemployment in the 1980s and 1990s, just as it had done in more extreme form in the 1930s. If it were true that there is a natural rate, episodes such as the monetarist experiment could easily be justified. Any recession or unem-ployment caused by contractionary policy will only be very short-lived, as market forces promptly return the economy to full employment. It might therefore be well worth going through the temporary inconvenience of a recession to secure the everlasting benefits of lower inflation. The problem is that things do not seem to work out this way in practice. Unemployment, in particular, in many jurisdictions has remained stuck at levels which would have seemed impossibly high, and even politically untenable, a quarter of a century earlier. Even where unemployment has come down fairly rapidly, as in the two most recent recoveries in the USA, this has apparently been simply a response to an explicit reversal or easing of either monetary or fiscal policy, as opposed to an 'automatic' rebound caused by market forces.

One response to persistent high levels of unemployment has been simply to assert that the natural rate itself had increased for a variety of exogenous reasons. This argument however, is something of an embarrassment for its supporters. For obvious reasons, the notion of a natural rate which does little more than track the actual unemployment rate is bound to be unconvincing (Solow, 1986). Theoretical reasons for hysteresis and persistence effects in unemployment rates have been advanced, and the idea that a policy induced recession will be quickly reversed by market forces is much less persuasive now than it once was.

THEORETICAL RESPONSES TO EMPIRICAL DIFFICULTIES

The empirical difficulties described above actually led to the demise of the most popular macroeconomic theory of the late 1970s in a remarkably short period of time. By the mid-1980s, McCallum (1986: 1) was able to refer uncontroversially to 'the recent downturn in popularity of the Lucas–Barro theory of cyclical fluctuations induced by monetary misperceptions'.

The difficulties of the more orthodox version of monetarism have also been widely discussed in the academic literature (e.g. B.M. Friedman, 1988; Goodhart, 1989), and even among economists who are supporters of monetarist or new classical views, there has been a willingness to re-examine the effectiveness of interest rate manipulation, rather than monetary targeting, as the direct instrument of monetary policy (McCallum, 1986; Barro, 1989a; Goodfriend, 1993). This is a change of some significance, as the direct use of interest rates as a policy tool had been more or less totally dismissed in academic discussion during the monetarist 1970s (Friedman, 1968; Sargent and Wallace, 1975).

In spite of the empirical failures, however, there is no sign that the enterprise of theory construction itself has suffered any sort of downturn. Snowden *et al.* (1994) have identified no less than seven main schools of thought in theoretical macroeconomics which were competing for attention in the mid-

1990s. In addition to (1) the orthodox Keynesians, (2) monetarists, (3) new classicals, and (4) Post Keynesians, the authors also discuss (5) a neo-Austrian school carrying on the traditions of Mises and Hayek, as well as (6) an updated version of orthodox Keynesianism which is labelled 'new Keynesian'; and, finally, (7) a later 'real business cycles' version of new classical theory.

It is clear why some version of orthodox sticky-price Keynesianism would enjoy something of a revival following the events of the 1980s and 1990s. After a series of policy-induced recessions, the traditional Keynesian could simply say 'I told you so', or its academic equivalent.

However, the mere correspondence between the short-run 'facts' and the short-run predictions of the traditional Keynesian model is ultimately not enough to win back the hearts and minds of professional economists. This is because of the continuing internal conceptual problem, from the point of view of mainstream economic theory, of justifying the key nominal rigidities within the standard theoretical framework. Therefore, to provide such a justification has become the self-appointed task of so-called 'new Keynesian' theory. Although the spectrum of recent work which might be included under this rubric is very wide, the most basic characteristic of such an approach is to search for the 'microfoundations' of the underlying wage or price rigidities in the attempt to solve the conceptual problems in a way consistent with the peer-defined technical standards of the day. If such a search was successful, the new Keynesian theory would have solved the empirical problems of new classical theory, and yet also avoided the theoretical stigma which has always been attached to Keynesian economics in the eyes of mainstream theorists.

One leading version of the new Keynesian approach combines the notion that firms in modern economies are likely to be price-makers rather than price-takers in product markets, with the observation that nominal product prices may be costly for these firms to change (Ball *et al.*, 1988). The so-called 'menu costs' of price changes may be small, but are significant enough at the individual firm level that it makes sense for firms to adjust their prices only at discrete intervals. The aggregation of such behaviour then leads to price rigidity at the macroeconomic level, allowing fluctuations in nominal aggregate demand to have real effects on output and employment. Due to demand externalities, even small menu costs at the microeconomic level can imply large output fluctuations for the macroeconomy.

Interestingly enough, however, in spite of their mathematical sophistication, the new Keynesian theories do not actually lead to a very much different view of appropriate macroeconomic policies than old-fashioned orthodox Keynesianism. Their contribution is entirely internal to the academic discipline of economics, in clearing up perceived conceptual difficulties. They are not at all closely connected with the alternative interpretation of Keynes discussed earlier. A more general rehabilitation of Keynes would have to get to grips with this set of issues also.

The other recent alternative theory mentioned by Snowden *et al.* (1994), 'real business cycle' theory, is a logical extension of new classical thinking. This consists essentially of updated versions of the venerable neoclassical growth model, in which aggregate output is determined by aggregate capital and labour inputs and the state of 'technology'. Profit-maximizing firms and utility-maximizing consumers choose optimal patterns of consumption, saving and capital accumulation as the system evolves through time. These models are driven by serially correlated shocks to the state of technical knowledge, which, so the adherents of these theories claim, induce dynamic patterns of behaviour (fluctuations as well as growth) in the theoretical models which are very like those of the real world.

One of the reasons for an immediate upsurge in popularity of the real business cycle models in academic circles is that they present no *conceptual* problems at all for economists schooled in the mainstream tradition. Expectations are rational, prices and wages are perfectly flexible, agents optimize and markets are perfectly competitive. It is for these reasons that real business cycle models can be presented as the immediate heirs of the earlier 'monetary misperceptions' new classical models, even though they are on opposite sides of another traditional dividing line in economics.

Nonetheless, however acceptable the real business cycle models may be from the conceptual viewpoint of standard economics, the empirical problems faced by this new approach are already sufficiently severe to call into question its staying power. Aside from the numerous technical criticisms which can always be made, two fundamental difficulties may be noted. The first point, made by several authors, is that a model in which shocks to technology are the driving force is hard pressed to explain recessions and depressions as well as booms (Greenwald and Stiglitz, 1988). How could the Great Depression of the 1930s be explained in these terms, for example? An even more significant difficulty derives from the original starting point of the real business cycle view, the denial of any causal role to monetary factors. Ironically, the first versions of real business cycle models appeared in the literature in the early 1980s (e.g. Kydland and Prescott, 1982) at a time when the consensus of most observers of the practical situation was *precisely* that changes in monetary policy were the key to current events. If practical policy applications were the driving force in the construction of economic theory (which they may not be), the timing could not have been worse to introduce a new theory with the message that money does not matter.

A monetary system and an account of the determination of nominal prices can be formally integrated into a real business cycle model in a manner which resembles the Post Keynesian view of 'endogenous money' (King and Plosser,

1984). This is another irony, as this perspective has usually been regarded with great suspicion by mainstream economists. The vision, however, is one in which the money and credit systems simply adjust passively to innovations on the 'real' side, and money exerts no independent effect.

MACROECONOMICS AND DYNAMICS

For the sake of completeness, a couple of other currents in contemporary mainstream macroeconomics, aside from those emphasized by Snowden *et al.* (1994), should be mentioned.

One such is a turning away from the debate over business cycle theory to deal with the problems of long-run economic growth. This is allegedly on the grounds that the latter are more important, but it must be said that there is also an air of relief on the part of orthodox theorists, in turning away from a debate in which the subject matter is not the natural domain of standard economics to one in which it is. The debate shifts to the safe ground of technical change and 'human capital' formation and away from the irritating topic of the neutrality or non-neutrality of money. A similar phenomenon was apparent in the 1950s and 1960s, after the original 'Keynes versus the classics' debates, when the relative merits of Harrod–Domar or Solow–Swan models in growth theory replaced the issues of the Keynesian revolution as the main topic for academic debate.

The more recent theories, as in Romer (1986), Lucas (1988) and Rebelo (1991) focus on self-perpetuating or 'endogenous' growth which results from either positive externalities in the formation of human and physical capital or increasing returns. The idea is to explain the obvious differences in growth rates between countries and why these seem to persist rather than converge. Even though, according to Robinson (1964: 98), the earlier work of Harrod (1939) had *already* 'set us off on a fresh line by treating technical progress as a built-in propensity in an industrial economy' the new work has been treated as a breakthrough, the point being that in the intervening 40 years or so 'the neo-classical doctrine that technical progress is…an occasional shock which shifts the equilibrium position of the system' (Robinson, 1964: 98) had once again been in the ascendant under the auspices of the Solow (1956) model.

A potentially more significant topic in economic dynamics which has also been a focus of recent academic debate is actually a questioning of the time-honoured division of the subject into separate branches dealing with growth theory, on the one hand, and the business cycle and stabilization policy, on the other.

The motivation for a reopening of the issue of the relationship between trend and cycle in the standard literature has come partially from technical developments in the analysis of time-series data, but also from empirical problems in reconciling the sluggish behaviour of unemployment rates (in Europe, in particular) with standard models of the business cycle.

In the traditional view, the issues of long-term economic growth and the business cycle were conceptually distinct. The underlying rate of economic growth could be explained only by real factors, the growth of the labour force, the accumulation of capital, technical progress, and so on. The function of macroeconomics, however, was at one time thought *not* to be to elucidate these issues, but rather to explain the observed fluctuation *around* trend known as the business cycle. It was in this context that the impact of changes in nominal aggregate demand, the effect of nominal rigidities, and the influence of rational or irrational misperceptions were supposedly relevant. There were fierce debates on these issues, but for a long time there was one issue on which all parties, at least in the mainstream schools of thought, seemed to agree. This was that whatever went on during the business cycle, and however long it lasted, the long-run growth trend of the economy would not itself be affected. Sooner or later the business cycle fluctuations would die down and the economy would revert to trend.

If it is believed that the trend growth rate is impervious to what happens during the cycle, this explains why policy actions such as the monetarist experiments of the 1980s could be undertaken with a clear conscience. No matter how bad things could get in the short-run, there was an underlying confidence that the pendulum would always swing back. Observed 'hysteresis' effects in unemployment rates during the most recent recessions have shaken this confidence, and a spirit of scepticism has been reinforced by the technical econometric evidence that key macroeconomic time-series do not necessarily exhibit a deterministic linear time trend. They can often be represented by so-called ARIMA (autoregressive integrated moving average) processes which can be decomposed into trend and stationary components, in which the trend is variable and can be represented as a 'random walk' (Stock and Watson, 1988). When a variable follows a random walk, its time path is determined by its value in the previous time period plus a random shock. The effects of any shock therefore spread themselves into the indefinite future. A negative shock decreases the current value of the variable, which then decreases the value of the variable in the next period, and so on, with the only offsetting factors being future random shocks. There is no 'steady-state' to which the value of the variable automatically returns, and hence the conventional picture, of an ultimate reversion to some well-established trend, is no longer valid.

The decomposition of time-series into trend and stationary components provides a number of technical questions for econometricians to debate, but what is important in the present context are the implications of the debate for the political economy of macroeconomic policy.

At one extreme, evidence for a quantitatively important random walk component might be interpreted as evidence for the real business cycle hypothesis. Observed fluctuations in economic growth might be mainly associated with a move from one trend growth rate to another, and the business cycle might be interpreted as primarily a side-effect of growth innovations. Such a view need not necessarily be synonymous, however, with the strict real business cycles view that *only* technological shocks cause growth innovations. At apparently the other end of the theoretical spectrum, the evidence might be construed as providing support for the Keynesian view that demand management may have significant long-term as well as short-term effects. The economy may not be able to bounce back after a downturn caused by a restrictive monetary policy, for example, and may be shifted to a permanently lower growth path.

A reconciliation of the two views (seemingly diametrically opposed) may ultimately be that the sensible macroeconomic policy is whatever is calculated to improve the average level of performance, and hence the trend growth rate. If this is done, the argument might go, the business cycle will take care of itself. A corollary would be to avoid the line of reasoning which seeks to deliberately slow down or depress economic growth for any reason (such as to cure inflation), as it cannot blithely be assumed that the growth rate will always bounce back to a healthy level via the operation of 'natural' forces.

CONCLUSION

As Keynes predicted long ago, it is obvious that the academic debate (and in the modern era this has primarily meant the academic debate in the USA), however esoteric and mathematically complex this may seem to be to outsiders, has greatly affected the climate of ideas around the conduct of macroeconomic policy, and has therefore directly impacted the real economic welfare of the population. In particular, contemporary attitudes which treat inflation as being of primary importance, and suggest that government policy can do little about such real problems as mass unemployment, except to the extent of improving the 'business climate', has had powerful support in the academic literature. There is a serious question, however, as to whether this scholarly effort has been well-directed.

NOTES

1. 'The cost of inflation', *The Economist*, 13 May 1995.
2. A. Coyne, 'Contrary to popular belief the conventional wisdom is sometimes right', *The Globe & Mail* (Toronto), 1 May 1995.

3. See also, Hodgson (1988: xi).
4. Or not, one is tempted to remark, reflecting on the conclusions which some of the most famous economists of our own time have apparently drawn.
5. Keynes, committing his famous 'solecism' (1936: 3, fn.) included *both* the genuine classical school of Smith, Ricardo, *et al.*, and the later 'neoclassical' school of Marshall and Pigou under this rubric. Historians of economic thought usually make a sharp distinction between these schools, and for some purposes this indeed would be essential (for example, in discussing the development of marginalism). However, it was perhaps not an unreasonable procedure for Keynes's purposes in discussing the macroeconomic and aggregative issues, on which the classics and neoclassics had very similar views. The contemporary new classical school seems to use the term classical in the same sense as did Keynes.
6. Cagan (1989) discusses the origins of the term 'monetarism', which he attributes to Brunner (1968).
7. The argument cited is explicitly based on evidence published in the earlier Friedman and Schwartz (1963) volume.
8. The adaptive expectations hypothesis was first introduced into the economics literature in the 1950s by such authors as Cagan (1956) and Nerlove (1958). It later became a mainstay of macroeconomic models of inflation based on the 'expectations-augmented' Phillips curve. Because of its *ad hoc* nature it became the first proximate target of the 'rational expectations revolution' engineered by the new classical school in the late 1970s and early 1980s.
9. As with the orthodox Keynesians it seemed to be taken for granted in this literature that the objective of policy was smoothing the cycle rather than improving the average growth rate. See, for example, the model presented by Sargent and Wallace (1975).

5. Inflation and the economy

INTRODUCTION

There is no question that for the past 15 or 20 years macroeconomic policymaking in the advanced industrial countries has been dominated by the fear of inflation. As discussed, this is essentially the legacy of the experiences of the 1970s when inflation rose dramatically in the G7 in a way which was unprecedented in peacetime or 'normal' conditions (Broadus, 1995). The overall average inflation rate in the G7 nations was around 8.5 per cent for the decade of the 1970s. Although this might not seem like a very large problem by the standards of some parts of the world, or other historical epochs, it was certainly enough to provoke major changes in attitudes in the case of North America, Western Europe and Japan in the modern era. Peak inflation rates were more dramatic, at more than 20 per cent in the case of Italy, Japan and the UK, and in double figures for Canada, France and the USA. Among the G7, only (West) Germany escaped double-digit inflation in the 1970s, and even this inflation experience was extreme by that country's own modern standards.

The argument put forward in this book is that we are still living with the consequences of the mind-set formed by policymakers during this period. It is true that inflation does slip off the immediate political agenda whenever it subsides for a while, but, on recent experience, it seems likely that the cycle of events which has already been repeated at least twice since the 1970s will re-emerge whenever the inflation statistics threaten to tick upwards once again.

THE CURE FOR INFLATION

The underlying theory of inflation held by the relevant policymakers during this period has been one variation or another on the theme of the ancient quantity theory of money, in its modern guise of monetarism. The theory asserts that an increase in the quantity of money will increase the level of money prices in the same proportion. Similarly, that an increase in the rate of growth of the money supply, allowing for changes in the rate of growth of the real economy, and adjustments to the velocity of circulation, will lead to inflation. In short, inflation is believed to be caused by a rate of monetary growth in excess of the rate of growth of the real economy. As the Friedmans (1980: 254) have put it: 'substantial inflation is always and everywhere a monetary phenomenon'. From this follows that the remedy or cure for inflation is apparently simple – the rate of monetary growth must be reduced.

The contribution of the twentieth-century monetarists was to persuade both academic economists and policymakers that, appearances to the contrary, it was possible to apply the logic of the ancient quantity theory even in the context of a contemporary credit economy in which the bulk of the money supply consists of the liabilities of financial intermediaries such as banks. The most obvious feature of this environment, as compared with a situation in which 'money' consists only of coins or fiat currency, is that the money supply will expand when bank lending increases and contract when the loans are repaid. Hence, if the monetary authorities are to conduct monetary policy and fight inflation according to the principles of the quantity theory, the question immediately arises as to how the central banks can exert control over this process.

According to monetarist theory, the answer was that the commercial banks would continue to need to hold reserves of the monetary base of the system, which in essence means the note and deposit liabilities of the central bank. Hence, the rate of growth of the money supply can supposedly be controlled by manipulating the rate of growth of the base, which then feeds through to the published monetary aggregates via the textbook 'money multiplier'. This in turn will control inflation. These ideas provided the basic inspiration for the monetary targeting experiments of the late 1970s and early 1980s, and also, albeit at one remove, for the later 'zero inflation' initiatives of the late 1980s and early 1990s.

However, 'base control', as it is known, did not work well in practice. For institutional reasons most central banks are unable to conduct monetary policy in the textbook monetarist fashion. Central banks can and do make use of their monopoly supply of base money to enforce a desired level of short-term interest rates in their respective jurisdictions (Goodhart, 1989; Goodfriend, 1993), but are reluctant to actually refuse to make reserves available on those terms. This is because of their responsibility for the liquidity of the system and the traditional 'lender of last resort' function (Moore, 1988). The short-term interest rate is then the effective policy instrument, and the central bank will have only indirect control over both the monetary base and the monetary aggregates as these adjust endogenously to different settings of the interest rate.

Also, in a period of rapid financial innovation the information content of the traditional monetary aggregates is drastically reduced, and it becomes unclear which of the statistically-defined aggregates, if any, corresponds to the theoretical concept of the quantity of money. The standard Friedman-type monetary rule therefore becomes untenable. Indeed, one of the main preoccupations of contemporary monetary economists has been to suggest some alternative, such as the targeting of nominal GDP, to achieve the same objective of controlling inflation (McCallum, 1995).

What 'tight money' seems to have meant in practice is, therefore, simply increases in short-term real interest rates, to whatever extent is necessary to restrain bank lending, provoke an economic slowdown, and then feed through to reductions in the inflation rate. In this way, even if monetarism *per se* was a failure, disinflation policy has usually been a success on its own terms. High real interest rates will succeed in reducing inflation. However, they only do so by causing a recession and unemployment, thus effectively disciplining those involved in the wage bargaining and price-setting process.

IS THERE A TRADE-OFF BETWEEN INFLATION AND UNEMPLOYMENT?

Mainstream economists, apart from some extreme believers in the policy irrelevance proposition some years ago, have usually accepted that there will be substantial negative side-effects to any attempt to reduce inflation. However, in response to this they have used the familiar slogan 'short-term pain for long-term gain'. In other words, the recession and unemployment required to reduce inflation are supposedly explicitly temporary, and it is worthwhile for society to bear the rigours of a short-term recession in order to reap the benefits of a permanently lower rate of inflation. This slogan is all the more attractive for the potential winners in that they are unlikely to be the same people who actually suffer the 'pain'.

Clearly the notion of short-term pain for long-term gain depends on the assumption that there is *no* long-run trade-off between inflation and unemployment, only a short-run trade-off. In terms of the theoretical Phillips curve, the assumption is that only the short-run Phillips curve has a negative slope, and that the long-run Phillips curve is vertical. Keynes (1923; 1971: 65) made a pre-emptive criticism of this type of thinking more than 70 years ago with his famous comment that 'in the long-run we are all dead'. Beyond this, however, recent experience must surely also have put a major dent in this conventional model of the economic process. The economic slowdowns and recessions required to reduce inflation to a low level seem to be much deeper and long-lasting, particularly in terms of unemployment, than could reasonably be described by the expression 'short-term'. As mentioned in the previous chapter, this has led to a new research area which investigates the reason for hysteresis and persistence in unemployment rates. It is also clear that recoveries from policy-induced recessions, when they do occur, do not come about 'automatically' as a result of pure market forces, but only after an explicit reversal of the original policy initiatives (Romer and Romer, 1995). Essentially, a decision (political or otherwise) is taken that the downturn has now proceeded far enough and that it is now safe to reverse course on interest rates.

Indeed, there is serious doubt as to whether either part of the slogan 'short-term pain for long-term' gain is accurate. The pain seems to go on for far too long, but also the 'gain', that is the perceived benefits of a lower inflation rate, is considerably less than permanent. Consider, for example, the situation in the industrialized economies in the 1980s. In most jurisdictions, as a result of severe recessions in the early part of the decade, inflation rates were substantially reduced (e.g. to around the 2 to 2.5 per cent range in North America) by the middle of the decade. According to textbook vertical Phillips curve theory, having gone through the pain, there should then have been no problem in resuming non-inflationary growth, and enjoying the benefits of a lower inflation rate for the rest of time. This presumption was actually the basis for claims that there will always be an enormous net pay-off to the whole society as a reward for enduring the rigours of disinflation policy (Feldstein, 1979). In the real world in the 1980s, however, inflation rates began to rise again *almost as soon* as the real economies began to recover in the later part of the decade. In other words, the lower rates of inflation lasted for only two or three years. This then led to arguments for a rerun of the whole disinflationary process, which in fact occurred in the early 1990s. Inflation came down once more, but as early as 1994 the US Fed was *already* worried about the possible resurgence of inflation yet again.[1]

And so on in an apparently endless circle. This depressing state of affairs seems inexorably to raise the awkward question of whether or not the only way to keep inflation down permanently is to have permanently high real interest rates and a permanently depressed economy. This is a suggestion which is apparently taboo in contemporary academic circles, but has been raised by some of those most directly affected by the policies. For example, in recent informational literature the CAW union in Canada has referred to the entire 1980–1994 period as a 'permanent recession' and presented figures on unemployment, growth and real wages to back up that claim.[2]

THE COSTS OF INFLATION

We are left with the question of just why it is that hardline anti-inflation policies have been in vogue for the past 15 to 20 years, and why the perceived problems caused by inflation have been taken so seriously that the monetary authorities have thought it justified to provoke two very serious recessions within a decade, simply in the effort to restrain cost pressures. Evidently, the threat of unemployment for workers, and bankruptcy for firms and many individuals, is now regarded as the only sure-fire way to ensure moderation in wage demands and the setting of prices.

The pain and suffering caused to millions of people by policy-induced recessions are presumably obvious enough, but what is less clear is the precise nature of the benefits to be gained by struggling through these desperately hard times simply to knock a few percentage points off the reported rate of change of prices. It is a serious question whether, in the Canadian context for example, life was better for most people in 1992 (with an inflation rate of 1.5 per cent and an unemployment rate of 11.3 per cent) or in 1979 (with an inflation rate of 9.2 per cent and an unemployment rate of 7.4 per cent). Yet such questions do not seem to get asked in esoteric academic discussions of rational expectations, policy rules, shifting Phillips curves, and the time-consistency properties of various dynamic models.

Professional economists, for the most part, have been amongst the most vociferous supporters of zero inflation policies, but have notably failed to give a clear and concise explanation, in common-sense terms, of just why it is that this particular economic statistic should take precedence over everything else. In fact, at first sight, an excessive concern with inflation seems to contradict one of the most basic economic principles taught in introductory courses, which is simply that dollar magnitudes in themselves have no particular economic significance unless they are related to some measure of purchasing power, that is how much those dollars will actually buy. The rate of inflation is defined as the rate of change of some index of the average dollar price of all goods and services. But if the prices of all goods and services, *including wages*, are going up at much the same rate, so that most people can continue to buy roughly the same quantity of goods even at higher prices, then it is hard to see exactly what is the problem in a moderately inflationary environment. Wage income, in particular, tends to go up at least as fast as the overall inflation rate (wage increases are often cited as the *cause* of a later increase in prices) and, if so, there is no reduction in the purchasing power of a given amount of work effort.

The chapters on the costs of inflation in economics textbooks are notoriously thin. The staple fare of 'shoe-leather costs', which would literally mean the cost of more 'trips to the bank' in the course of managing one's financial affairs in an inflationary environment, and 'menu costs', meaning the physical resource costs of changing price lists and menus, were always unconvincing. They have become even more so in today's increasingly electronically-based credit economy. Smithin (1990, 1994a) provides a detailed critique of the textbook arguments.

A more practical and hard-headed argument that inflation has substantial social costs (and hence the corollary that disinflationary policies may be worthwhile) would focus on the view that the uncertainty and confusion caused by unanticipated inflation is likely to hamper economic efficiency, damage productivity, and reduce economic growth. If there is uncertainty about the future course of prices, this is presumed to adversely affect individual decisions made about saving, consumption and investment. As in the worst nightmares of the neoclassical economist, resources will be 'misallocated'. However, there is actually very little concrete empirical evidence that moderate inflation seriously affects productivity and growth. *The Economist* newspaper recently published a 'scatter diagram' showing the average rates of inflation and growth for 20 countries over the period 1960–90. This was based on academic research by Barro (1995).[3] If there really was some long-run negative relationship between inflation and growth, uncontaminated by short-run Phillips curves showing the opposite relationship, then surely it would show up here? It turns out, in fact, that there is almost no discernible relationship. Some countries had higher than average inflation *and* higher than average growth, others had lower than average inflation and lower than average growth, and there is every other conceivable combination in between. Obviously, the main determinant of long-run growth is something other than a nation's inflation experience. *The Economist* goes on to argue that a scatter diagram, as such, does not provide much useful information and that much more sophisticated statistical analysis is required to uncover the 'true' relationship. However, it also reports Barro's research on a 100 country sample which itself does not provide strong support for the view that there is a quantitatively important relationship between long-run inflation and long-run growth. They are wrong, moreover, that a scatter diagram provides *no* useful information. If there is no relationship between average inflation and long-run growth discernable in the basic data, it at least shows that a single-minded 'zero inflation' policy provides no guarantee of any eventual improvement in growth. Many countries which have actually *achieved* lower than average inflation over a long period have also been stuck with lower than average growth. Similarly, high inflation has been no barrier to high growth in many other cases.

The journalist Linda McQuaig (1995), presents a critique from a common-sense point of view of the widely-cited study by Jarrett and Selody (1982), and of later policy recommendations based on these results. This study had found a strong negative relationship between inflation and productivity growth based on Canadian data from the 1970s. It is true, of course, that both high levels of inflation and the infamous productivity 'slow-down' did occur simultaneously in that decade, but McQuaig's point is that the coincidence of timing does not necessarily establish any causal connection between them. Logically, if productivity growth slowed *because* inflation was high in the 1970s, it should have improved dramatically when inflation was reduced to much lower levels in the 1980s and 1990s. But obviously this did not happen.

However, there clearly must be a powerful constituency which is very much in favour of policies designed to lower inflation. Otherwise there would hardly be such a formidable apparatus, including central banks, international institutions, academic economists and financial journalists continuously arguing in its favour. The key is that there are also distributional consequences of inflation, particularly an inflation which is imperfectly anticipated. In such a case, the real rewards of economic activity will be distributed differently from what would have occurred if there had been no inflation. This will be regarded as unfair by those who lose and as a windfall by those who gain. The mere fact that the outcome is different than expected may well increase social tensions even if there are as many winners as losers, and the redistribution of income will also have effects on economic incentives.

Economic theorists are not usually comfortable with applying the principle of *cui bono*? (who gains) to explain economic events. The more usual vision is of a monolithic 'public interest' in which everybody apparently will be a winner from whatever policy position is being advocated. However, in the case of inflation and disinflation, and failing any other rational explanation, it seems to be absolutely necessary to work out who are, or will be, the winners and losers, if any progress is to be made at all in understanding the process. This is the procedure advocated by what Palley (forthcoming) calls the 'new structuralist' school of economists, even if it is usually anathema to standard economic reasoning.

THE POLITICS OF ANTI-INFLATION POLICY

Having broached the topic of income distribution, it is then really not that difficult to establish where the main source of support for deflationary policy must lie. Self-evidently the main purpose of anti-inflation policies is to preserve the value of money; therefore the main beneficiaries must be those individuals and institutions who already possess a large quantity of that particular asset, that is the wealthy financial or rentier interests. To anyone whose 'net worth' is zero or worse, which apparently applies to 55 per cent of the US population, for example, the value of money as such can hardly be relevant to his or her well-being (Greider, 1987: 39). On the other hand, it *is* highly relevant to the top 2 per cent of households who own 54 per cent of total net financial assets, and the top 10 per cent who own 86 per cent of the total. Note that if the vehicle for achieving price stability happens to be high real rates of interest then so much the better for the so-called rentiers.

One of the best discussions of the distributional consequences of unanticipated inflation remains that by Keynes in the first chapter of his *Tract on Monetary Reform* (1923; 1971) published more than 70 years ago. In the *Tract* Keynes examined the effects of an unanticipated inflation on three classes or strata of society, the 'investing class' (rentiers or financial capitalists), the 'business class' (entrepreneurs, manufacturers and merchants) and the 'earner' or workers. The hardline methodological individualism of contemporary neoclassical economics is supposed to preclude any modern approach to an economic problem along these lines. According to the methodological purists, for the discussion to be valid it must always lead back to the isolated individual or 'economic agent' who has immutable tastes and preferences, and makes all the relevant economic decisions. Keynes however, anticipated the neoclassical objection that the threefold class division of income does not necessarily correspond to the individual distribution. He conceded that 'the same individual may earn, deal and invest' (1923; 1971: 4), but none the less thought that there was something to be learned by investigating the effect of inflation on the different income sources, particularly in terms of the effects on the incentives to engage in each type of activity. In contemporary society, the class divisions suggested by Keynes may well be obsolete, with the role of the investing class, for example, played by the pension funds and other institutional investors and that of the business class by large corporations. None the less, we can still follow Keynes's logic on the effects of inflation on the incentives for the provision of financial capital, the organizations of productive activity, and the supply of work effort, respectively. In addition to the obvious point that the activities of dealing, earning, and investing are not of equal importance in every individual's life, the question of incentives remains the crucially important issue, regardless of which side of the political fence one is on.

Keynes's major point was the familiar one that an unanticipated inflation redistributes income and wealth from creditors to debtors. If outstanding debts are denominated in terms of nominal dollars, pounds, or yen, an inflation reduces the real value of that debt, benefiting the debtor, and for a given nominal yield the real value of interest payments on the debt is reduced also. Keynes could see some benefits for society as a whole (obviously not for the creditors) in such a transfer, in the sense that debtors tend to be the 'active' part of the community (e.g. farmers, merchants or manufacturers) who have borrowed to set the productive process in motion, whereas the creditors are 'inactive' (1923; 1971: 8–9). None the less, and there is some irony in this given the reputation he would later have in monetarist circles, he felt that inflation as such was an inefficient way of achieving this transfer. There should be (1923; 1971: 16–17):

other ways...[of adjusting]...the redistribution of national wealth, if, in course of time, the laws of inheritance and the rate of accumulation have drained too great a proportion of the income of the active classes into the spending control of the inactive.

Governments also are frequently debtors and historically their desire to also acquire more purchasing power has been one of the main motives for the pursuit of inflationary finance; the so-called 'inflation tax'.

The main worry which Keynes (in 1923) had about a redistribution away from the investing class was that it would remove the incentives for saving and capital accumulation, which he felt had been the cornerstone of Victorian prosperity (1923; 1971: 4–17). This was the view of a pre-*General Theory* Keynes, of course. The later Keynes would have had investment leading to savings, rather than the other way around, and would therefore presumably have been less worried about anything which weakened the motives for saving, and more in favour of a transfer of income to those who would be more likely to invest.

The effects of inflation on Keynes's other two classes, meanwhile, are much more benign. The business class of entrepreneurs actually benefit, not only because the real value of their outstanding debt decreases (assuming them to be typically the debtor class), but also from the fact that the rise in prices makes it easy to make profits, as their goods-in-process appreciate on their hands. This argument depends on the assumption that the nominal interest rate does not rise sufficiently to compensate for the increase in inflation, otherwise a simple rise in the nominal prices of goods-in-process obviously will not lead to an increase in real profits. To put the point another way, the assumption is that the *real* interest rate falls. This draws attention, or should do, first to the assumption that the inflation rate under consideration is not fully anticipated, or, and perhaps more to the point, even if it is so, that it is not possible for creditors to be fully recompensed; and second, to the vital importance of the behaviour of the real, rather than the nominal, interest rate.

Keynes also felt that wage-earners do not suffer very much from inflation, the argument being that labour unions are usually able to secure rises in nominal wages which at least compensate for the inflation. During an infla-tionary period there is little resistance on the part of employers, whose profits are rising anyway, to nominal wage increases (1923; 1971: 25–8).

In addition to the point about the disincentive effects on capital accumula-tion, however, Keynes also felt that even if the inflation is not actually reducing the real wages of labour, it will none the less cause social stress because of perceived injustices (1923; 1971: 32). Hence, in spite of any temporary stimulus to output that an unanticipated inflation may cause, the Keynes of the *Tract*, surprising though it may seem to conservative econo-mists of the present day, was essentially making the case that price stability (zero inflation) was the most sensible goal for public policy to aim at. As with other economists writing about the same time, however, it must be borne in mind that these views were being put forward in the early 1920s, when the impact of inflation, coming immediately after the Victorian era of price stability, was much more of a shock to contemporaries than any inflationary experience in the late twentieth century could be. Even though Keynes used his discussion of the impact of inflation on different 'classes' to ultimately advocate zero inflation, therefore, it will nonetheless be suggested here that a similar framework can be used to explain *both* why there has been a resurgence of interest in the same goal in the present day, and also why these policies may not ultimately succeed even in their own terms.

The explanation for the renewed focus on disinflation, and more particularly zero inflation, both in rhetorical discussions of macroeconomic policy and actual decision-making in recent years, can then be explained in terms of a political shift away from both labour *and* business, and in favour of finance. Here we are using the term 'business' to apply to those firms engaged in actual productive activity, the contemporary counterpart to Keynes's 'business class' of manufacturers and merchants; while 'finance' means the contemporary institutional counterparts of Keynes's 'rentiers'. And, as a matter of fact, the symptoms of this shift can be seen everywhere in contemporary discourse on economic and financial matters. These include the arguments in favour of the 'independence' of central banks from the control of democratically elected governments, the push towards a single currency and a supranational central bank in Europe, and the concept of the 'inflation scare' as the primary motivation for changes in the conduct of macroeconomic policy in general (Goodfriend, 1993; Broadus, 1995). There is also the simple fact that real interest rates in most jurisdictions have been in the order of 4 to 5 percentage points higher in the 1980s and 1990s than in the 1950s, 1960s and 1970s.[4] As discussed in some detail by Greider (1987), the symbolic turning point in this political process was the appointment of Paul Volcker as chair of the US Fed in 1979. This appointment was made by the Democratic President Jimmy Carter under massive pressure from banking and financial interests in the United States. This immediately resulted in a leap in real interest rates in the USA (and hence the world) from near-negative levels in the late 1970s to almost record levels by the early 1980s.[5] Note that this also gives us some hint that the real point at issue is not so much inflation *per se*, but the degree of protection which is afforded to accumulated financial wealth at any point in time.

INFLATION AND INTEREST RATES

As mentioned earlier, in the credit economy, the money supply, on whatever definition, will expand or contract with the volume of lending by financial intermediaries. In this environment, descriptions of monetary policy changes along the lines of Friedman's famous 'helicopter', showering the landscape with banknotes like manna from heaven, are clearly less than adequate. The natural way of thinking about monetary policy is now in terms of a comparison between the rate of interest charged by the banking system on money loans and the rate of return to be earned by employing the borrowed funds in various types of productive activity. This differential will provide the incentive or disincentive for other agents to become indebted to the banking system, and hence the impetus for the money supply to expand or contract. In the history of economic thought, the analysis of the credit money system was associated, in particular, with the work of Thornton (1802; 1962) and Wicksell (1898; 1965) in contributions published almost a century apart. Both made monetary analysis hinge on a comparison between the interest rate charged by the 'Bank' and the rate of return to be earned in productive activity, with bank lending (and bank liabilities) adjusting endogenously. The key assumption made by both Thornton and Wicksell, however, and by many writers down to the present day, was the existence of what Wicksell was to call a 'natural' rate of interest. This is a hypothetical rate of interest that is supposedly determined in principle by the equivalent of barter in the capital markets, and which cannot be changed by monetary manipulation. Any attempt to set the actual bank rate different from the natural rate is then supposed to lead only to inflation or deflation. If the bank rate is set 'too low' this provides an unlimited incentive to borrow and hence leads to inflation, conversely 'too high' a bank rate would lead to deflation. This way of thinking therefore neatly combines a discussion of inflation with an implicit warning against any attempt on the part of central banks and governments to interfere with the verdict of 'market forces' as to what should be the real rate of return on financial capital. This 'Wicksell–Thornton' way of looking at things (Smithin, 1994a), no doubt seemed very old-fashioned at the zenith of influence of the monetarist school and the new classical school around 1979–82. More recently, however, given the breakdown of the monetary targeting experiments, there is evidence that central banks in general, and the US Fed in particular, have essentially reverted to a focus on achieving the 'correct' level of short-term real interest rates as the implicit monetary policy rule. The Fed under Alan Greenspan in the 1987–95 period, for example, seemed to conduct monetary policy via interest rate manipulation according to a rule which would keep the real Federal funds rate at about 2 per cent, which was believed to be consistent with a long-run inflation rate also of 2 per cent (Judd and Trehan, 1995; Taylor, 1993).

Although to revert to this quasi-Wicksellian type of procedure may well be an improvement, in some respects, over the simple monetarist-type rule which was the fashion some years before, there are still some severe difficulties with the 'natural rate' theory of interest which underlies it. As discussed in detail by Smithin (1994a) the natural rate theory is not particularly plausible in a genuine credit economy, or what Keynes called a 'monetary production' economy (Asimakopulos, 1988). It amounts to assuming that a unique real rate of interest is determined on barter capital markets in which savings are somehow embodied in heterogenous concrete physical commodities and can be traded to investors for use as capital goods in specific production processes (Rogers, 1989). Furthermore, that this already unrealistic picture is in no way altered by the actual historical development of monetary payments systems and sophisticated credit facilities.

As argued by Smithin (1994a), an apparently much more reasonable conception for the monetary production economy would be that the rate of interest is determined in the first instance in the monetary or financial sector, and that rates of return elsewhere must adjust to this standard rather than vice versa. In a monetary system those responsible for setting production in train, whether they are entrepreneurs or corporations, must first acquire monetary resources, by borrowing, selling equity, or previous accumulation, before they can do so. The ultimate proceeds of productive activity are also sums of money. Intuitively, therefore, and contrary to the point of view that money does not matter, in such an environment the general operation and efficiency of the monetary system, and, in particular, the terms on which the monetary resources necessary for production are obtainable, would seem to be of vital importance. In a monetary economy, both the type and scale of projects to be undertaken, and hence the macroeconomic rate of return on those projects, will be determined in a fundamental way by the cost and availability of finance, which must be arranged before production can commence. Therefore, if the monetary authorities engage in interest rate manipulation in order to impact the rate on inflation, they cannot, or at least should not, be so confident either that their efforts will have no impact on the real economy, or, if they do so, that these effects will only be short-lived.

This is actually a very ancient debate in monetary economics, although the point seems to have been entirely glossed over or avoided in mainstream contemporary theoretical and policy discussion. The opposing points of view were very concisely put in a posthumous 'exchange' (separated by 119 years) between Ricardo and Keynes, as appended by Keynes to chapter 14 of his *General Theory* (1936). Ricardo, though failing to develop his monetary economics in as much detail as in the earlier work of Thornton (1802; 1962) or the later contribution of Wicksell (1898; 1965), was none the less able to put the conventional theory in a nutshell in the following passage from his *Principles of Political Economy* (1817; 1973: 246):

> with respect to the interest for money; it is not regulated by the rate at which the banks will lend, whether it be 5, 4, or 3 per cent, but by the rate of profits which can be made by the employment of capital, and which is totally independent of the quantity or value of money. Whether a bank lent one million, ten million or a hundred millions, they would not permanently alter the market rate of interest; they would only alter the value of the money which they thus issued...The applications to the bank for money...depend on the comparison between the rate of profit that may be made by the employment of it and the rate at which they are willing to lend it. If they charge less than the market rate of interest, there is no amount of money which they might not lend; if they charge more than that rate none but spendthrifts and prodigals would be found to borrow of them.[6]

To which Keynes (1936: 191) had the following equally clear reply:

> Ricardo and his successors overlook the fact that even in the long period the volume of employment is not necessarily full but is capable of varying, and that to every banking policy there corresponds a different long-period level of employment; so that there are a number of positions of long-period equilibrium corresponding to different conceivable interest policies on the part of the monetary authority.
>
> If Ricardo had been content to present his argument solely as applying to any given quantity of money created by the monetary authority, it would still have been correct on the assumption of flexible money-wages. If...Ricardo had argued that it would make no permanent alteration to the rate of interest whether the quantity of money was fixed by the monetary authority at ten millions or a hundred millions, his conclusion would hold. But if by the policy of the monetary authority we mean the terms on which it will increase or decrease the quantity of money, i.e., the rate of interest at which it will...increase or decrease its assets – which is what Ricardo expressly does mean... – then it is not the case...that the policy of the monetary authority is nugatory or that only one policy is compatible with long-period equilibrium...Assuming flexible money-wages, the quantity of money as such, is indeed, nugatory in the long period; but the terms on which the monetary authority will change the quantity of money enters as a real determinant into the economic scheme.

So the basic issues have been debated for some time, even if they have been ignored in the recent mainstream theoretical debate.

THE REAL ISSUE?

Returning to Keynes's three social groups or 'classes' we can see that the impact of inflation on each is intertwined with that of changes in the real rate of return on financial assets. These occur as part and parcel of the attempts to change the rate of inflation in either direction by monetary policy.

For example, Keynes's 'business' class, or industrial capital, is not really adversely affected by inflation as such, because their goods-in-process appreciate on their hands. Logically, though, they should have a very keen interest in the real rate of interest at which they can finance their activities. Recall that for there to be any genuine profiteering from inflation, the real rate of interest must actually fall. Otherwise, in a continuing production process, refinancing next period's production at new higher prices will eat up whatever nominal profits are gained from selling today's finished goods at similarly high prices. A high real rate of interest, on the other hand, the by-product of any attempt to bring inflation down, will be to the disadvantage of this group, for two main reasons. First, an increase in real interest rates directly increases their financing costs, prohibitively so for 'marginal' projects. Second, the impact of higher real interest rates on economic conditions generally, by causing a downturn in overall economic activity, will also adversely affect profitability.

Labour, also, it was suggested, can cope reasonably well with inflation as such, but will suffer from attempts to reduce it via deliberately created downturns caused by high real interest rates. There will be *both* unemployment and lower real wages.[7]

On the face of it, therefore, there is a divergence of interest between labour and industrial capital on the one hand and financial capital or the rentiers on the other (Palley, forthcoming). The former groups have no real problems with moderate inflation, and do require an expanding economy and relatively low real rates of interest in order to prosper. The rentiers or financial capitalists, however, seem to have economic interests which may be directly opposed to those of the other two classes in this respect. They are adverse to inflation as such, because of the impact on the real value of wealth accumulated in the form of financial assets, and are not really adverse to the classic remedy for inflation, which is high real interest rates (except possibly in individual cases of an inappropriately-timed bond market speculation). The influence of real interest rates on rentier welfare goes even deeper than this, however, because, as long as the *real* rate of return on financial assets is positive, even an agent who has maintained the bulk of his/her wealth in assets denominated in terms of the national currency is effectively indexed for inflation. Very few such individuals or institutions, after all, really do keep a substantial quantity of the proverbial 'banknotes under the mattress'. They would doubtless always prefer a higher real rate to a lower, but as long as real rates remain positive by even a small margin, then at least the accumulated real value of financial assets is maintained. The ultimate disaster for the rentier is when real rates of return on financial assets become negative. In this case, there is literally no way to maintain the value of accumulated wealth by financial investments. The only way to maintain the value of wealth would be to get out of financial assets entirely and into something like real estate. But, during the stagflationary 1970s, negative real rates of interest did become a reality, or a serious threat, for many investors. By making this point we can immediately gain a deeper level of insight into the political economy of that decade than just by focusing on inflation alone. Not only was there inflation, but there was also *little protection* from inflation for an influential and power-ful group within the society. It is not really surprising, in retrospect, that there would then emerge powerful political forces for change.

Before leaving the topic of who gains what from variations in the inflation rate and real interest rates, two further points should briefly be mentioned. One is that in terms of the rhetoric which is employed in the political arena to justify 'tight-money' anti-inflation policies, it is more usual for the politicians to invoke the problems of persons with limited means and on fixed nominal incomes, such as pensioners. They do not focus on the need to preserve the real value of accumulated financial wealth. However, if the former really was the main item for concern it could presumably be dealt with simply by passing legislation that pension incomes etc., should be indexed to some measure of the cost of living (Smithin, 1990, 1994a). This would certainly create less difficulties for the society as a whole than the disinflationary methods which have actually been used. Moreover, McQuaig (1995: 139) points out that in Canada, which was one country in which indexation of state pensions was already in place, there were moves towards *de-indexation* dur-ing precisely the same period when inflation was supposedly a major policy concern. This hardly indicates that the welfare of pensioners is the main priority of élite politicians.

A more substantive issue is that although frequently the representatives of industrial capital or 'business' do protest about negative effects of the impact of tight-money policies in the public arena,[8] they are also sometimes found to be 'onside' with the financial agenda of low inflation, high interest rates, and so on. This might be explained by a simple lack of rationality on the part of the spokespersons involved, but, more likely, it reflects the fact that reces-sions and unemployment are not always or initially unwelcome from the business point of view. The argument would be that a recession would disci-pline the workforce, and make them less likely to push for real wage in-creases. Hence, the implicit goal may be to increase real profitability by the cost-cutting route (Stanford, 1995). The problem with this argument, how-ever, is that business profits also decline, and business bankruptcies increase, when aggregate demand is low and there is a severe recession. The goal of 'disciplining the workforce', therefore tends to have aspects of a self-defeat-ing strategy, certainly when pushed too far. It is literally a question of 'cutting off one's nose to spite one's face'. As Palley (forthcoming) explains the point in a formal model, in reality the preferences of labour regarding unemployment and inflation are likely to be at one extreme, and those of finance at the other, with those of business somewhere in the middle. Thus, according to Palley:

> The fact that financial capital has a stronger interest in low inflation and high unemployment than does industrial capital, means that these two interest groups can part ways, leaving open the possibility of an alliance between labour and industrial capital.

The longer a downturn persists, therefore, the more likely it seems to be that the 'business class' will break ranks with the representatives of finance on the crucial issue of monetary policy.

THE 'REVENGE OF THE RENTIERS'

In re-examining the macroeconomic trends discussed in chapter 2 in the light of the ideas presented in this chapter, the 'good years' for the advanced industrial economies in the 1950s and 1960s can now be interpreted in essence as having been something of a grand compromise between the competing interests. This ultimately worked out to the benefit of all. Presumably, the reason that the compromise could be made to stick at that time was simply the lessons of experience delivered by the disasters of the first half of the twentieth century, the Great Depression and two world wars.

In any event, the 1950s and 1960s were both an era of relatively cheap money (Kaldor, 1986) and also (conscious or unconscious) efforts on the part of those responsible for macroeconomic policy to maintain the pressure of aggregate demand. It was an era of fixed exchange rates (albeit subject to periodic changes) under Bretton Woods, so that US monetary policy, whatever that happened to be, would be transmitted to the rest of the world system via the exchange rate regime. The upshot was a period of strong growth, high employment, and increases in both real wages and business profits, which would clearly be of benefit to both Keynes's 'business' and 'earning' classes. The cost was a moderate inflation, but this seemed to be of remarkably little concern to anyone at the time, even the 'investing class' or rentiers. The point was that although real interest rates were low (say no more than the 2–3 per cent range in many jurisdictions) they were at least positive, and hence the value of accumulated financial capital could at least be maintained. This then was the nature of the implicit compromise, and even if the financial interests were not necessarily receiving top dollar for their investments, the situation presumably seemed to be a reasonable trade-off after the drastic instabilities of earlier in the century.

The compromise came apart, of course, during the years of 'stagflation' in the 1970s. The various objective problems of that decade, such as the aftermath of the Vietnam War, the break-up of the Bretton Woods system, and the oil shocks, were converted into a generalized inflation, as policymakers around the world simultaneously took the opportunity afforded by the floating exchange rates to pursue actively expansionary policies. They took seriously the 'pop' Keynesian remedy of spending one's way out of economic difficulties, and pursued a 'cheap money' strategy with a vengeance. The notorious 'Barber boom' in Britain in the early 1970s (Smith, 1992: 14–16), named after the then Chancellor of the Exchequer, was a classic example of this, as an irresponsibly expansionary policy led first to rapid growth but later to record inflation. These events had their counterparts in many other jurisdictions.

The key thing about the attempted cheap money policies of the 1970s, as opposed to their more successful counterparts of the previous decades, is simply that caution was thrown to the wind, and real interest rates actually became *negative*, or close to it, at times. Nominal rates may have seemed quite high, as compared to earlier years, but this was quite definitely illusory. If the nominal interest rate is 15 per cent say, and the inflation rate is around 20 per cent and is expected to continue in that range, the real rate is actually *minus* 5 per cent. The borrower is actually being *paid* for borrowing, and the lender is, in effect, expropriated. From the point of view of the borrower, the name of the game is simply to borrow *ad infinitum* – there is no way to lose. This unlimited incentive to borrowing will obviously make the inflation situation get further and further out of hand. Superficially, this may seem to be a good thing from the point of view of the 'business' and 'earning' classes. It becomes seemingly easy to make profits and gain wage increases. This may be most apparent to the average citizen in a rapid appreciation of the real estate value of the family home, as did in fact occur in the 1970s. However, unlike the more stable situation of the 1950s and 1960s, where real rates were low but positive, it is doubtful if capitalism as we know it is actually viable on these terms.

The ultimate incentive system under capitalism, is, after all, the accumulation of financial wealth, and if this is inevitably going to be expropriated by negative real rates of interest, that incentive system will break down. Currently struggling entrepreneurs and workers may well get a boost from a negative real rate in the short term, but what will then happen when they themselves have become successful in accumulating some wealth? If they are to be expropriated also, or can only hold on to their wealth by continued frantic activity in the real estate market or other schemes, the incentive to engage in economic activity in the first place may wane. The 'ideal' capitalist incentive scheme, presumably, would indeed make it relatively easy to get into the game, via cheap loans and buoyant markets, but would also provide some guarantee that one can hold on to one's gains once they have been achieved. Negative real interest rates may help with the first of these requirements, but not with the second.

In any event, the situation of the 1970s was not politically stable, and there was indeed something of a political revolution around 1979–82, the main aim of which was to place the main focus on the preservation of the value of financial assets as the purpose of public policy, rather than other goals such as full employment. The modern development of mainstream economic theory, particularly in the élite schools in the USA, as described in detail in chapter 4 above, was itself a major factor in this development.

The events of the 1980s and 1990s, therefore, which have seen the playing out of this revolution, can be described rhetorically as the 'revenge of the rentiers' (as opposed to the 'euthanasia of the rentiers' looked forward to by Keynes). If public policy blatantly neglected the concerns of financial capital in the 1970s, the exact opposite has been true in the 1980s and 1990s. The policy agenda and priorities of central banks, governments, and international agencies have been primarily concerned with financial rather than real variables. The public rhetoric has focused in particular on three such variables – inflation, budget deficits, and the exchange rate – each of which is discussed individually in the present volume. The real impact of the changing policies, however, has been to accomplish a shift to a regime in which, on average, real rates of interest are persistently much higher than in earlier years.

These results are good for the rentier interests in the short term, just as the 1970s were bad for them, but the real economy unfortunately suffers. There is low growth, low real wages, low profits in the industrial sector, and unemployment. In effect, it can be argued that the reaction in the 1980s and 1990s, to the problems of the 1970s, was one of 'overkill'. Real interest rates may have dropped to low and even negative levels in the 1970s, but this has more than been made up for in the two decades since. There is a contradiction, however, in the too aggressive pursuit of policies favouring the financial interests, even from the point of view of the potential beneficiaries. Ultimately, money itself is only valuable in as far as it represents a valid claim on the flow of goods and services produced by the real economy. The problem is, therefore, that policies designed to benefit the already-rich and the financial sector, when pushed to their logical conclusion, simply end up by depressing the real economy on which everybody's livelihood ultimately depends.

The obvious remedy for these difficulties, or so it would seem, is to return to something more akin to the 'compromise' of the 1950s and 1960s. There could be cheap money in real terms, but finance would get its reward as long as real rates were not allowed to become negative as in the 1970s. At the same time there would still be enough 'space' for the rest of the economy to grow. Unfortunately, a return to this type of compromise currently seems unlikely, given the apparently limited understanding of the issues on the part of those currently responsible for economic policymaking. The debate is carried on the context of overly simplified models of the economic process, which actively avoid discussion of the most important issues at stake. For this, the contemporary economics profession does bear a heavy burden of responsibility.

CONCLUSION

The most salient feature of the 'capitalist' economic process, which seems to be lost in the contemporary focus on the supposedly damaging effects even of moderate inflation, is that the most progressive and dynamic elements in the economy at any point in time, those on whom future growth depends, tend to be those firms and individuals who have *not* already made a fortune, and are hungry for success.

A budding entrepreneur, for example, who has a bright idea for some new product or service, but little initial capital, will need to borrow from a bank or other financial intermediary to pay for the wage bill, capital equipment and raw materials. Success will depend on the price of the final product being *high* enough not only to repay principal and interest on the initial loan but also to yield some reasonable rate of profit. The entrepreneur has to worry not only about the rate of interest that is charged but also the price that is eventually received. If prices in general are falling over time, even if this is desirable from the point of view of those who already have financial resources, entrepreneurship obviously becomes a rather dubious proposition. Even if prices are only rather flat, which is actually the goal of zero inflation policies, it seems that our entrepreneur's life will still be something of a struggle.

At the other extreme, when there is positive inflation, and if the interest rate which is charged is not enough to compensate lenders for the increases in prices that are occurring (that is if real rates are negative), what is actually happening is that the existing rich are being quietly dispossessed of their fortune for the benefit of the up-and-coming generation. This may not be fair, but it might be argued that the latter group, after all, are the ones whose activity is most likely to get the economy going.

At some points in history, indeed, this type of logic has been pushed to extremes. In Bolshevik Russia after 1917, for example, Lenin deliberately used the weapon of hyperinflation to wipe out the resources of the middle class. In a functioning market economy, though, there must obviously be some limit to an inflation-led redistribution of wealth, if only for the reason that the ultimate objective of today's penniless but dynamic entrepreneur is also eventually to become as rich as the previous generation. As discussed above, if the redistribution process becomes too obvious, the incentive system breaks down, and there would be no point in the new participants entering the capitalist struggle, even on initially very advantageous terms. Vigorous anti-inflation policies, on the other hand, requiring very high real rates of interest, are in essence simply a case of the rich getting richer. They tend to shut the real economy down, prevent the new generation from getting started, and tip the balance too far in the direction of the dead hand of the past. It is this which has actually been the express goal of policy in most of the industrialized nations for the past two decades. The most reasonable conclusion to draw, surely, is that it would be better to strike some kind of balance, which preserves existing wealth, but at the same time does allow some scope for new sources of wealth to develop.

The truth of the matter is that there may never be a completely satisfactory solution to the problem of inflation, as such. This is simply because, contrary to the views of the more dogmatic textbooks, there are actually many different potential sources of inflationary pressure and it may not always be feasible to fully offset all of the possible shocks which can hit the economy. A policy, therefore, which *always* advocates sacrificing the real economy whenever inflationary pressures develop, simply to preserve the wealth of those individuals or institutions who have already achieved economic success, stands a very good chance of eventually ending up by impoverishing the whole society.

However, if it is recognized that the real point at issue is not simply the values of the arbitrarily calculated inflation statistics in themselves, but the need to maintain a reasonable balance between the claims of existing wealth and the demands of the future, there clearly is a policy which may achieve this. It is the opposite of those actually pursued in many jurisdictions over the past several years, but may none the less be successful. This is simply that the objective for central banks should be to stabilize after-tax real interest rates at low but still positive levels (say no more than 1 per cent or 2 per cent), rather than focusing on particular targets for either the inflation rate or the rate of growth of the money. This would avoid the damage to the real economy caused by the very high real rates which have precipitated recent recessions, and, although it might not squeeze all inflationary pressures out of the system, it would at least avoid the additional boost to inflation which occurs when real rates are allowed to become negative as in the 1970s. Under such a regime, the already-rich may not become very much richer, but, as long as real returns remain positive, at least they would not suffer the erosion of capital which was the original source of anti-inflationary agitation.

NOTES

1. See 'Much ado about nothing', *The Economist*, 26 March 1994.
2. See *Economic and Social Action: Facts and Figures for the Frontlines*, CAW/TCA Canada, July 1995.
3. See 'The costs of inflation', *The Economist*, 13 May 1995, p. 78.
4. See *Economic and Social Action*, July 1995, p. 6. In the Canadian case, the short real rate is estimated to have averaged only 1.1 per cent in 1950–80 compared to 6.1 per cent in 1981–94, while the average real rate paid by the government on the national debt rose from 3.9 per cent in 1950–80 to 7.7 per cent in 1981–94.
5. On the crudest measure of real interest rates, that is subtracting annual average inflation rates from annual average nominal interest rates in the same year, real short rates averaged 6.3 per cent in the USA, 7.5 per cent in Canada, 8.1 per cent in West Germany, and 4.4 per cent in Japan by 1981. Given that inflation was actually falling between that year and the next, in three of the four jurisdictions (it did not change much in Germany until later), plausible forward-looking estimates for annualized real rates could be much higher.
6. Obviously, Ricardo means by 'market rate' much the same thing that Wicksell later called the 'natural rate'.
7. As is well known, it is not true, as Keynes (1936: 17–18) had originally thought, that real wages move countercyclically.
8. Palley (forthcoming) gives the examples of the CBI in Britain, and certain US industrialists who supported President Clinton in the 1992 US election in the USA.

6. Cause and effect in the relationship between budget deficits and the rate of interest

INTRODUCTION

As illustrated by the case of inflation, discussed in the previous chapter, one of the most disturbing traits of contemporary politicians and commentators on economic affairs is the tendency to periodically zero in on one or another of the multitude of economic statistics that are available and to make that the exclusive focus of their concern for the time being, neglecting everything else. This is no doubt a lot easier than actually thinking about the difficult issues of economic policy-making, and would probably be harmless if it could be confined to political speeches and party conventions. It can become positively dangerous, however, when politicians in power actually try to take decisions on this basis that affect the well-being of ordinary people.

Although there may be no *apparent* logic to the particular choice of 'economic numbers' which are attracting attention at any point in time, there is nonetheless these days, a common theme. It seems to be always the purely financial variables which mainly concern the policymaker and the 'markets', and rarely the economic indicators relevant to the well-being of the average citizen, such as jobs or real wages. If wages go up, for example, this is more likely to be criticized by financial commentators for making the economy 'uncompetitive'.

Second only to inflation, as the subject of fashionable concern, would be the nominal dollar magnitudes of annual government budget deficits and the accumulated national debt. Moreover, worries about budget deficits and debt always seem to surface at what an earlier, more 'Keynesian' generation of professional economists would have regarded as the worst possible time, such as in a recession. This is a problem, because the actions needed to achieve serious deficit reduction, such as increases in taxation, or drastic cuts in government spending, or both, are the opposite of what common-sense would prescribe for an economy which is already in difficulties, in which unemployment is high, and growth is low. Yet, the 'populist' vision of stringent retrenchment and budget cuts inevitably seem to suggest itself as a remedy at just these difficult times, as indeed it did in the 1930s.

Writing some years ago, Coddington (1983: 1–5) suggested that one of the most important distinguishing characteristics of old-fashioned Keynesian economics, broadly defined, was that it encouraged a 'utilitarian' perspective on public finance. That is to say, the state of the public finances was to be judged not by purely internal criteria, such as the concept of 'sound finance', but by the impact of budget decisions on the economy as a whole, particularly on the variables most relevant for economic welfare. As pointed out earlier, Keynes's own main policy proposal in *The General Theory*, the 'socialization of investment' (1936: 378), was not primarily concerned with short-term fiscal policy or budget deficits (Kregel, 1985; Pressman, 1987; Smithin, 1989; Seccareccia, 1993). Nonetheless, for the world at large, it probably is fair comment that one of the by-products of the discussion of Keynesian ideas in the first few decades after World War II was at least to modify conventional ideas of financial probity as applied to the public accounts.

In the present era, however, this point of view appears to have been almost entirely rejected by policymakers in many jurisdictions, under the influence of both the current generation of academic economists and the pressure of events. As pointed out by Parguez (1993a: 6–7), there has been a reversion to the attitudes traditionally exemplified by the so-called 'Treasury View' in Britain in the 1920s and 1930s (H.M. Treasury, 1929).

The purpose of this chapter is to critically examine these attitudes towards budget deficits, in the light of both theory and recent experience.[1] It is argued that the popular 'doomsday' scenarios depend on a theory of interest rate determination, and a view of the interaction between monetary and fiscal policy, which is not really plausible in a credit economy, in which the money supply is endogenous, and the rate of interest is determined primarily by the policy decisions of the central bank. In particular, in this environment the causal relationship between interest rates and deficits is probably the reverse of what is usually suggested. That is, high real interest rates may be the cause rather than the consequence of high debt and deficits. The problem is then that an austerity policy designed to cut deficits and reduce debt may simply become a self-fulfilling prophecy, essentially *imposing* ex-post an 'economics of scarcity' (Parguez, 1993b) which is the assumed starting point of the standard analysis.

THE BURDEN OF GOVERNMENT DEBT AND DEFICITS

Thirty years ago, Robinson (1964: 71) could write of the Treasury view that '(n)owadays this seems merely laughable', but such sixties sentiments would obviously be very out of place in the current climate. The views of the most influential decision-makers have apparently now come full circle, with much of the contemporary policy debate based on what Modigliani (1983: 59) once dismissed as the 'naive burden' approach. This relies on simplistic (and misleading) analogies to the finances of the individual household. In this type of argument, exclusive emphasis is placed on nominal deficits and the accumulation of nominal debt, regardless of the ratios of these magnitudes to nominal GDP, comparisons with past historical experience, or the phase of the business cycle. Even relatively straightforward measurement issues, such as those stressed by Eisner (1986, 1989)[2] are frequently ignored. Although such views may not stand up to elementary economic analysis, they nonetheless remain influential, and do have real economic consequences resulting from attempts to put them into practice.

In the background, moreover, there is also a 'sophisticated burden' view (Modigliani, 1983: 61) which similarly fuels concern about the scale of debt and deficits. This is probably ultimately even more important, in that it provides the imprimatur of economic analysis for actions taken by policy-makers on more instinctive grounds. This more sophisticated argument is nothing other than the familiar 'crowding-out' hypothesis, of which two main versions are advanced. In the closed economy context, increased real borrowing by the government supposedly competes with the private sector for a fixed pool of savings at each income level, and hence drives up real interest rates and crowds out productive private investment spending. In this case, the burden of increasing debt is believed to be a smaller capital stock and a lower standard of living bequeathed to future generations. Alternatively, in the small open economy with flexible exchange rates, the argument is that the domestic rate of interest must eventually adjust to the level determined on world capital markets and that incipient upward pressure on domestic rates therefore leads primarily to currency appreciation. In this case, it is the export and import-competing industries that are crowded out (Gray, 1987). In a large open economy, such as the USA, some combination of the two effects is expected (Yellen, 1989: 18). These are the primary arguments which lead many economists, as opposed to politicians, also to be suspicious of budget deficits and to the advocacy of harsh austerity measures.

ALTERNATIVE THEORIES OF INTEREST RATE DETERMINATION

Implicitly or explicitly, most economists have a heuristic understanding of the crowding out analysis based on one version or another of the 'loanable funds' theory of interest rate determination, which, in an earlier generation, was associated with Robertson (1934). We are therefore back to the vexed question of interest rate determination which has already been raised in earlier chapters. In the orthodox loanable funds theory, the (real) rate of interest is determined by the interaction of the net flow demand for loanable funds (for investment and other purposes) with the flow supply of new savings. The intersection of the demand and supply schedules determines something similar to Wicksell's (1898; 1965) 'natural rate' of interest. This equilibrium rate is supposed in principle to be a 'real' phenomenon, representing the true underlying economic motives of the borrowers and lenders, and hence is impervious to manipulation via the monetary policy actions of central banks.

The impact of additional borrowing by the government would be to shift outwards the demand schedule for real loanable funds and drive up the natural rate of interest. If the incentives for private investment spending are otherwise unchanged, the new higher rate of interest means that less private investment expenditure is forthcoming, even though the total volume of borrowing, including government, has increased. Presuming that the displaced private investment would have been more productive than government spending, the impact will therefore be to reduce capital formation and retard future economic growth. The underlying assumptions of the theory are that the money supply is exogenously fixed, and that investment cannot proceed unless an appropriate amount of savings is already in place to finance it.[3] As in the classical theories of saving criticized by Parguez (1993b) and Seccareccia (1993), savings lead to investment rather than the other way around. On these assumptions an increased demand for the use of savings on the part of government is bound to mean that there will be less available for private investment spending. Even though, given a conventional upward-sloping savings schedule, a higher rate of interest will induce potential savers to devote a somewhat greater amount of available resources to saving rather than consumption, this will not be enough to fully accommodate the increased demand and hence there must be a smaller volume of savings available to finance private investment.

One of the main objectives of Keynes's *General Theory* was to challenge this conventional theory of interest rate determination. According to Keynes's theory of 'liquidity preference', interest rates are determined not by the interaction of the flow demand and supply schedules for new borrowing and lending but by the relative demand for a given quantity of money and the stock of alternative financial assets ('bonds'). This, in turn, depends upon the strength of the various 'incentives to liquidity' (1936: 194–209) including the 'speculative motive'. For Keynes, interest rates were essentially a monetary phenomenon, determined in the money markets, and the direction of causality between the monetary economy and the real economy was explicitly reversed.

However, if this critique of the accepted theory of interest rates was one of Keynes's main intended messages, it is obvious that the so-called Keynesian revolution did not succeed. The mere fact of the renewed prominence of the crowding out doctrine is in itself sufficient indication that the pre-Keynesian view of the determination of interest rates is once again a key component of both macroeconomic theory and the conduct of fiscal and monetary policy. As far as Keynes is concerned, most economists today believe that Keynes's main argument was that nominal wages can be 'sticky'. For example, 'new Keynesians' pay little or no attention to Keynesian interest rate theory, and many may not even have heard of it.

There is also a second 'Post Keynesian' theory of the rate of interest, which is much simpler, namely that the short rate of interest is essentially an exogenous policy-determined variable administered by the central bank. This is a view associated with the work of the Post Keynesian 'horizontalists' (Moore, 1988; Kaldor, 1986; Lavoie, 1992a) and also that of the 'circuit school' (Graziani, 1990; Parguez, 1993b; Lavoie, 1992b; Le Bourva, 1992). This point of view takes more seriously the concept of a credit economy, and Keynes's own idea of 'monetary production', than did the model which eventually appeared in *The General Theory*. In such an environment, the money supply consists primarily of the nominal liabilities of financial inter-mediaries, such as banks, and expands or contracts endogenously with the volume of bank lending. The rate of interest is determined primarily by the policy decisions of the central bank, by virtue of its position as lender-of-last-resort of the ultimate reserve asset of the system, and investment decisions can precede savings because of the availability of credit finance.

Some of the horizontalist authors, indeed, are critical of the original Keynesian liquidity preference theory, on the grounds that it assumes a fixed exogenous quantity of money, somewhat similar to the conventional monetarist view (Kaldor, 1986: 21–4; Moore, 1988: 171–208). On the other hand, the endogeneity of the money supply in the horizontalist literature arises because central banks, committed to preserve the liquidity of the financial system, are obliged to provide the necessary reserves to support an increase in the demand for credit, albeit at a price of their own choosing. In partial support of this point of view, it is noteworthy that economists with some knowledge of the institutional realities have usually confirmed that this is a reasonable description of the way in which real world central banks operate in practice (Goodhart, 1989: 208–9; Goodfriend, 1993: 3–5).[4] Moreover, although some economists, such as Wray (1992: 13–21), in an attempt to reconcile endogenous money with Keynesian liquidity preference, have suggested that the supply curve of money should be taken as positively-sloped rather than horizontal, the latter position is persuasively defended by Lavoie (1992a: 197–203).[5]

v for the crowding-out thesis and the debate over
e obvious. The main point being that, neglecting
for the moment, interest rates are fixed in place
s of the central bank, rather than by anything to
mporary conditions, moreover, it seems clear that
the short rate of interest should be thought of as
gh the monetary policy instrument is the nominal
an and do form expectations about the inflation
the nominal rate they will therefore be well aware
x-ante real rate, defined in terms of the expected
the estimates of their forecasting departments
e of a central bank, these forecasts would presum-
us of informed participants in other sectors of the
eminated would actually play a large part in shap-
er players. The 'real' rate thus established would
al rate estimated by average opinion and would be
relatively p...... impact of economic activity.

Also, in the absence of a natural rate of interest, it can be argued that
central bank control over short real rates will ultimately influence the entire
structure of interest rates in the economy, including long rates (Moore, 1988;
Lavoie, 1992a; Smithin, 1994a). According to the 'expectations' theory of the
term structure, the long rate is simply a reflection of the expected future time
path of short rates. In practice, this obviously allows for a wide range of
possible outcomes for the yield curve, depending on what expectations actually are. If long rates stay low when short rates rise, for example, or vice
versa, this may simply reflect the fact that the change in short rates is only
expected to be temporary. Nonetheless, the implication is that, in principle, a
sufficiently determined and consistent policy by the central bank regarding
real interest rates will eventually achieve its objective, whatever that happens
to be. Eventually, the real economy must adjust to the policy-determined
interest rate, rather than vice versa. This is therefore the precise opposite of
the natural rate doctrine. A role for Keynesian liquidity preference can be
retained in this scenario, in that liquidity preference considerations may well
periodically insert a wedge between those rates of interest which are more or
less directly under central bank control and rates elsewhere (Lavoie, 1992a).
This would certainly allow an indirect influence of budget deficits on some
interest rates in the system, due to nebulous changes in 'confidence', *but*
these effects would be explicitly temporary.

The general upshot of this approach would be that, given a firm stance on
interest rate policy by the central bank, and even in the closed economy or
large economy context, it would not be sensible to worry about crowding out
effects via the impact of budget deficits on the rate of interest. Up to 'full

employment' the impact of fiscal policy changes on output and employment would then be basically as suggested in the simple 'hydraulic' models of textbook Keynesian economics. Moreover, at the high levels of unemployment prevailing in most of the industrialized nations at the time of writing, the prediction would be that any concerted and successful attempt to impose an austerity agenda would actually significantly worsen economic conditions (Tobin, 1993: 15). There would be no appreciable effect on the rate of interest, except possibly by a later explicit monetary policy-induced response to the deteriorating situation. It goes without saying that the worsening of economic conditions would damage the prospects for capital accumulation rather than the reverse.

THE CROWDING-OUT HYPOTHESIS IN THE OPEN ECONOMY

In the open economy context, the potential impact of domestic budget deficits is frequently inferred from the so-called Mundell–Fleming or IS/LM/BP exercises of the textbooks. An expansionary fiscal policy, again against the background of an exogenously fixed money supply, supposedly causes an incipient increase in real interest rates as in the IS/LM diagram. Under flexible exchange rates the currency then appreciates and the resulting damage to both export and import-competing industries effectively offsets the original fiscal stimulus, and eventually restores real rates to the 'world' level. This is what is described as 'open economy crowding out' in the literature (Conklin and Sayeed, 1983; Gray, 1987).

At one time, interestingly enough, this type of analysis used to provide the basis for the argument that a supposedly 'Keynesian' fiscal policy would be effective *only* under a regime of fixed exchange rates. The argument was that with a commitment to a fixed parity, and given a similarly expansionary fiscal policy, as in the flexible rate case discussed above, the monetary authorities would be forced to buy foreign exchange (sell their own currency) and thus provoke a monetary expansion in tandem with the fiscal stimulus. This in turn was supposed not only to moderate the incipient rise in interest rates, but also to provide an additional *boost* to output and employment (rather than the opposite). As mentioned, however, it is likely that even this limited argument that budget deficits may not always be undesirable would be regarded as totally unacceptable to many decision-makers in the contemporary climate. The point would be that the expansion would be regarded as only a short-term phenomenon by believers in a 'natural rate' of both unemployment and interest.

As suggested by Smithin and Wolf (1993), the key point in the Mundell–Fleming scenarios is once again the view which is implicitly taken of interest rate determination. Either of the two alternative, and actually more 'Keynesian', views mentioned above would predict a different response to fiscal policy changes in the open economy, under either flexible or fixed exchange rates. Real interest rates would be held in place either by the state of liquidity preference, or simply the policy actions of the central bank, and hence would not be affected, even in the initial stages of adjustment, by fiscal policy changes. In the flexible exchange rate case, a fiscal expansion would then cause the currency to *depreciate* rather than appreciate, because of the operation of the import multiplier. The depreciation in turn, however, would tend to improve export performance and offset the original balance of payments difficulties *without* choking off the boom, as opposed to the crowding-out prediction of the Mundell–Fleming model. In contrast, in a fixed exchange rate regime the depreciation could not occur and, unless the other players were also pursuing a similarly expansionary policy, the expansion would tend to come to a halt in the face of balance of payments problems. In fact, this is what invariably happened during the Bretton Woods era whenever one of the smaller nations attempted a fiscal expansion at a greater pace than that of the system as a whole. Another possible example of this would be the events in France in the early 1980s, when membership of the exchange rate mechanism (ERM) in Europe was the key factor in what is usually cited as a famous policy 'U-turn'.[6]

It is this type of consideration which has lead Smithin and Wolf (1993) to argue that all versions of 'Keynesian' policy in a single jurisdiction seem to require some freedom of action on exchange rates. This is so regardless of whether Keynesian policy is construed as simply a cheap money policy involving monetary policy action to lower real interest rates; as the long-term policy of the 'socialization of investment'; or, more conventionally, as short-term fiscal policy. As illustrated on several occasions (including the relatively recent events surrounding the crises in the ERM in Europe in 1992 and 1993) fixed exchange rate regimes effectively block policies designed to stimulate growth or relieve depression in the individual jurisdictions, unless the policies of the leading player or 'key currency' nation allow for them. This issue is discussed in greater detail in chapter 7 below.

BUDGET DEFICITS, INTEREST RATES AND INFLATION

As for empirical evidence, Barro (1989b: 48) points out that in spite of the popularity and widespread acceptance of crowding-out scenarios, the formal econometrics literature actually provides little or no empirical evidence of any causal relationship running from budget deficits to either real or nominal interest rates, even in the case of a large open economy such as the USA. In

Barro's discussion, this is used as an argument in favour of the validity of the hypothesis of 'Ricardian equivalence', according to which an increase in the deficit will simply cause an increase in savings equal to the present value of the expected future tax bill eventually required to close the gap. Hence the deficit, as such, will not put upward pressure on interest rates. The Ricardian equivalence argument, of course, is often dismissed by rival economists as requiring an implausible degree of foresight and intergenerational altruism on the part of economic agents (Yellen, 1989: 19–20). However, the evidence cited by Barro is clearly also relevant to the more general position that interest rates are determined essentially independently of fiscal policy as discussed above.

It is not really necessary, moreover, to resort to econometrics to establish support for the view that there is little or no relationship between the size of the budget deficit and real interest rates, or at least not the relationship the standard theory would predict. This much is obvious on even the most cursory reconsideration of recent economic history. In the familiar North American case, for example, real interest rates were already very high in the early 1980s, when general government budget deficits were still relatively low, and then later tended to *fall* as budget deficits as a percentage of GDP were rising (due to Reaganomics) in the mid-1980s. In the later 1980s, real rates began to rise again well before budget deficits did, and then *fell* in the early 1990s as budgets deficits were rising. The obvious conclusion to draw, is that the behaviour of interest rates is driven primarily by monetary policy rather than fiscal policy. Specifically, the two periods of particularly high real interest rates in North America, in the early 1980s and early 1990s, obviously coincided with the two separate attempts at disinflationary 'tight money' policies on the part of the relevant central banks in 1981/82 and 1989 to 1991.

Another point which is obvious from recent basic data is that there is very little evidence of any association between budget deficits and inflation. This is another potential problem which has often been cited (in addition to crowding-out arguments) in the effort to generate public concern about deficits. The supposed relation between budget deficits and inflation, which had a number of influential adherents in both academic and political circles in the late 1970s and early 1980s (Smithin, 1990: 44–5), was dubbed 'unpleasant monetarist arithmetic' by its supporters (Lucas and Sargent, 1981). It was suggested that persistent budget deficits would, more or less inevitably, be eventually monetized via direct bonds sales to the central bank. Hence, according to the quantity theory of money they would then lead to inflation. In practice, however, there was, if anything, a negative correlation between budget deficits and inflation in North America in the 1980s and early 1990s. Deficits were at their highest when inflation was at its lowest, and vice versa. In the Canadian context, in particular, it should be noted that the much vaunted 'zero inflation' environment of the early 1990s coincided precisely with a period of mounting and vocal political concern about the size of both Federal and Provincial budget deficits.

THE RELATIONSHIP BETWEEN MONETARY POLICY AND FISCAL POLICY

It therefore appears that both theoretical considerations and (formal and informal) empirical evidence indicate that the relationship between such variables as the inflation rate, the real rate of interest, and the budget deficit, is actually essentially the opposite of that set out in the conventional literature.

It can be suggested that a stylized interpretation of the course of economic events which has been repeated in several jurisdictions over the past 15 or 20 years would *begin* with the apparently single-minded concern with inflation on the part of politicians and policymakers at the end of the 1970s, and only *end* with the equally obsessive concern with deficit reduction which became so striking in the public debate at a later stage.

As discussed in chapter 5, according to the monetarist version of the quantity theory of money, which was at its zenith in terms of political influence in the 1970s, the only way to reduce inflationary pressures was for central banks to reduce the rate of growth of the money supply. Due to the practical difficulties of monetary targeting, however, what has actually occurred in practice is that central banks have taken whatever actions were necessary to drive up real interest rates, and attempt to reduce inflation via the direct impact of recessions on wage and other cost pressures and profit margins. A sufficiently draconian policy will reduce inflationary pressure for a time, but only at the cost of large reductions in output and employment, and it may well be that inflation can only be permanently kept down by this method if the economy is kept permanently running at less than full capacity. In terms of the present discussion, the point is that these episodes of monetary policy-induced recession have had a direct impact on the fiscal situation and, hence, on public perceptions of the seriousness and urgency of the debate over debt and deficits.

The impact of deflationary policy on the government budget deficit is twofold. First, high interest rates themselves directly increase interest payments on the public debt, and the interest cost component of the annual deficit, both in absolute terms and as a proportion of the total. This leads immediately to the concerns which have become such a staple of discussion in both the financial and popular press, lamenting the rising proportion of each tax-dollar which is devoted to interest payments rather than the financing of public services. The obvious response to this would be for ministers of finance to instruct central bank governors that one of the tasks of monetary policy should be to ensure that the public debt is funded as cheaply as possible. Indeed 50 years ago, this was precisely how central banks saw their role in financing World War II, apparently with complete success (McQuaig, 1995: 220). However, this inference seems rarely to be drawn in recent commentary. Instead, one is more likely to read editorials extolling the virtues of the 'political independence' of central banks, so that they need not cooperate with the ministry of finance at all.

Second, monetary policy-induced recessions also increase measured budget deficits via the operation of what used to be described as 'automatic stabilizers'. In the former 'Keynesian' days, the so-called automatic stabilizers were thought to be a good thing. A reduction in income inevitably reduces the tax base for any given tax rate schedule and, therefore, total tax collections, while recessionary economic conditions simultaneously tend to increase mandated transfer expenditures, such as unemployment benefits. In other words, there is inevitably a tendency for government deficits to increase in a recession. This used to be thought desirable, as it would help to maintain the level of aggregate demand and hence offset the original deflationary pressures. Many contemporary governments, however, seem to have reverted to the pre-Keynesian view that recession-induced deficits require still *further* retrenchment, involving still more drastic cuts in government spending or large tax increases. According to the earlier understanding of these things this type of response would have been regarded as tragically perverse. Depending on the phase that the business cycle had already reached, they would cause either a worsening of the recession or at least the retardation of an incipient recovery. The contractionary policies may well not even achieve their announced objective of balancing the budget. A further slackening of economic growth simply further reduces the tax base, and increases the demand for welfare payments and unemployment benefits. To the extent that this type of policy response has now become the norm once again, either via 'balanced-budget' legislation or simply tacit acceptance of the new rules of the game, it may well become apposite to describe the contribution of fiscal policy as an 'automatic *de*-stabilizer' rather than a stabilizer.

The direction of causality suggested here, therefore, runs from concern over inflation in the wake of the inflationary decade of the 1970s, through very high real rates of interest, as a result of the attempts of key central banks to deal with this problem via monetary policy, and on to large measured budget deficits. These are caused both directly, as a result of higher financing costs, and indirectly because of the monetary policy induced recessions. Austerity policies to deal with the budget deficits then threaten to exacerbate the situation in a further downward spiral.

As in the case of inflation policy, Smithin and Wolf (1993) and Smithin (1990, 1994a) have suggested that a starting point for a more sensible and stable fiscal policy would also be for the monetary authorities to attempt to stabilize real interest rates at low but still positive levels, noting that this would only be feasible for an individual jurisdiction (in a situation where the policy responses of its trading partners cannot be guaranteed) if real exchange rates were also free to change. This is a pragmatic proposal based on the twin ideas that, on the one hand, high real rates reduce economic activity but, on the other, a policy which aimed at keeping real rates permanently *negative* would likely exacerbate inflationary pressures because of the unlimited incentive for nominal borrowing. The proposal would avoid the destabilizing fluctuations in real interest rates which have plagued many national economies over the past two decades, and hence represent possibly the best contribution that central banks could make to the maintenance of fiscal responsibility.

OPTIMAL FISCAL POLICY

A more stable interest rate structure, and the accompanying greater stability of output and employment, would make the formation of fiscal policy and budget planning a less hazardous exercise. It would avoid at least some of the distortions which have been observable in several jurisdictions in recent economic history. The ideal situation would be one in which taxation and transfer spending decisions can be made ultimately only in terms of the principles of social choice, rather than either the perceived requirements of macroeconomic policy or some arbitrary principles of financial accounting.

A number of authors (Kregel, 1985; Pressman, 1987; Smithin, 1989; Seccareccia, 1993) have also suggested that more attention be paid to the composition, rather than simply the volume, of government spending. In particular, the argument has been made that there should be more emphasis on the potential contribution of public investment spending (broadly defined) both to the maintenance of an adequate level of aggregate demand and the future growth of productive capacity. This is a view which has more in common with Keynes's actual policy proposals in *The General Theory* than the short-term fine-tuning which is often described as Keynesian policy in the textbooks.

In this regard, note that the concept of a separate capital budget for the public finances would turn the standard analogy to the finances of an individual household on its head. Although it might be reasonable to agree with the usual opinion that it is not sensible for an individual household to go into debt to support extravagant consumption expenditure, it is surely *not* appropriate to raise the same objection to household deficit financing of its investment or capital spending. Major financial decisions such as taking out a mortgage on a home or financing higher education would be the obvious examples. But the same argument should apply to government investment spending also. As far as the capital budget is concerned, therefore, the analogy between governments and households actually works in the *opposite* direction to the 'naive burden' view (Smithin, 1989: 214). In fact, it is highly unreasonable to argue, as is implicit in the deficit accounting of many jurisdictions, including Canada, that government capital spending should all be 'written off' in the current year. This would never occur in standard accounting practice in the private sector. In any event, whether investment takes place in the public sector or the private sector, a lower real interest rate policy would make all desirable investment spending less costly and hazardous, and hence make it more likely that it will actually be undertaken.

Although the argument in this chapter has stressed the causality running from changes in interest rates, and changes in output and employment, to budget deficits, rather than the reverse, this is not meant to imply that discretionary changes in tax and spending parameters have not also been important; one obvious example in recent economic history being the large tax cuts in the early Reagan administration in the USA in the 1980s. As suggested by Smithin (1990) these tax cuts, although justified by supply-side arguments, may well have had their primary impact on the demand side and represented a sort of inadvertent short-term Keynesianism. The discretionary element of US budget deficits was therefore arguably one of the factors responsible for the strength of the US recovery of the mid-1980s compared with that of Europe.

Nor is there any intention to deny that in general the overall size and composition of the public sector, and the size of the tax burden, are legitimate and important subjects for public debate. It may well be the case that at least some of the outcry over debt and deficits in recent years has arisen precisely because various fiscal policy decisions have been taken which are unpopular in themselves. For example, a government spending programme may be perceived to unfairly benefit one special interest group at the expense of another. Or, a programme may also simply be regarded as undesirable *per se* by many of those involved. These cases could range from the commonplace sort of issue where, for example, a major highway is driven through a residential neighbourhood, to questions involving deep philosophical differences between an unpopular government and its citizens. Similarly, the tax burden itself may be regarded, and presumably frequently is, as onerous or unfair in its incidence on the individual level. In any of these circumstances, the argument that 'we simply can't afford it' may actually seem to be the least-cost political method of getting rid of the undesirable programme. Pursuing this logic, a 'self-imposed' austerity, caused by policy-induced recessions and a deliberate running of the economy at less than full capacity, may even be regarded as a necessary evil in some quarters to 'prove' to the populace that one particular programme or another can no longer be afforded.

This is ultimately a self-defeating attitude, however, for the economy as a whole. In reality, many more programmes would probably be 'affordable' if appropriate policies were being pursued to restore full employment. This should not, however, prevent society from none the less making hard choices as to what is or is not actually desirable *in itself*, regardless of whether or not it can be afforded. In essence, what is happening is analogous to an individual quitting a well-paid and otherwise enjoyable job, and remaining unemployed, in order to remove the temptation of spending his or her money unwisely. It would be better to develop some will-power.

The arguments presented here also imply that the appropriate time to address the difficult issues of public choice is when economic growth is satisfactory and aggregate demand is buoyant (Tobin, 1993: 17–18). In other circumstances, during periods of substantial excess capacity and high unemployment, it is the aggregate demand implications of current levels of government spending and taxation which come to the fore. As pointed out by Goodwin (1988: 143) the logic of constrained optimization does not apply when resources are idle and the constraints are slack. Even if money is 'wasted' in some absolute moral sense, it may still be better to spend than not to spend from the point of view of society as a whole. This was the point made by Keynes (1936: 129–30) in his ironic discussion about providing employment by filling 'old bottles with banknotes' and burying them at a suitable depth for private enterprise to dig up. The point is not that more useful employment could not be found for those digging up the bottles, but that resources may as well be used for this purpose if they are not being used for anything else. Similarly, even though this may be of little consolation to the irritated customer in the post office, the efficiency or otherwise of the public service is less important, in times of depression, than the continuing contribution to aggregate demand made by the incomes received by public employees. This elementary logic, however, has apparently been forgotten by many contemporary politicians in government whose remedy for high unemployment and a lack of consumer demand is to add the names of some of their own employees to the unemployment rolls and, if possible, to cut the wages of those remaining.

CONCLUSION

If, in a world of sophisticated banking and financial systems with endogenous money, interest rates are not primarily determined by the demand for and supply of loanable funds, and investment spending is not constrained by a pre-determined fixed pool of savings, then it seems that the traditional crowding-out analysis of budget deficits has little theoretical force. Also, there is not much empirical evidence to support it. If anything, and with reference to recent events in a number of jurisdictions, it can be argued that high real interest rates are frequently a *cause* rather than a consequence of budget difficulties.

Contemporary concerns over the nominal dollar size of debt and deficits are therefore probably best seen as a further manifestation of the recent general tendency in macroeconomic discussion and debate to focus on the outcomes for nominal variables, such as the price level, nominal wages and nominal exchange rates, rather than real variables such as output, real economic growth and employment. As discussed in earlier chapters, this trend has gathered force since the 1970s, with the predictable result that performance in terms of the latter variables has deteriorated very considerably since that time. In this light, all such financially-based policy proposals, whether for zero inflation, nominal budget balance or debt repayment, or a rigid adherence to nominal exchange rate parties, can be seen simply as related aspects of what is essentially the same underlying approach to the basic problems of political economy. The objective is ultimately to preserve the value of existing financial wealth rather than to create new wealth.

From the point of view adopted in this book, this approach is based on a flawed understanding of the way in which the macroeconomy actually works, and is unlikely finally to be successful even in terms of its own objectives. As a result, considerable damage has already been done to the real economic prosperity around the world during the years in which these views have been in the ascendant. As in the case of inflation, so in the case of budget deficits, the best alternative advice to be given to current policymakers would be that they abandon the exclusive emphasis on purely nominal and financial variables which has been adopted in recent years. They should pay more attention to common-sense policies designed to improve performance in terms of the real economic variables which are relevant to the welfare of their constituents – real interest rates, employment, output, and real incomes.

NOTES

1. The chapter is based primarily on material published earlier in Smithin (1994b).
2. These would include potential inflation adjustments and 'par-to-market' adjustments in addition to 'structural' adjustments for the state of the economy.
3. Professor Alain Parguez has suggested to the author that even in the earliest versions of the crowding-out hypothesis, advanced in the 1920s, there was confusion between the concept of a fixed supply of money and a fixed supply of savings determined by prior accumulation. In the textbook IS/LM exposition, interestingly enough, the argument is based entirely on a fixed supply of *money* for transactions purposes. There is complete crowding out if there is zero interest elasticity of both money demand and money supply, and 'partial' crowding out if there is some interest elasticity of either money demand or supply. In this case, 'savings' concepts seem only to come in rhetorically, in explaining the argument to non-specialists in informal settings.
4. Goodfriend (1993: 6), however, would deny that the central bank can affect real rates, as opposed to nominal rates, on anything other than a temporary basis.
5. The basic argument is that although there may be subjective limits to bank lending, reflected in higher interest charges or credit rationing, at the microeconomic level of the individual bank and individual client, the same restrictions do not apply to the overall system expanding in concert.
6. Note, however, that Parguez (1993a: 17–19) questions the conventional interpretation that *discretionary* fiscal policy in France was expansionary at the time, even though the actual deficit did increase. The argument is that the stimulus to the economy came through a combination of the relaxation of previous efforts to inhibit the operation of the automatic stabilizers and a somewhat easier monetary policy. In any event, exchange rate problems led to an abrupt reversal of whatever degree of stimulus or relaxation had been in place, and a return to strict austerity policies.

7. What should be done about the balance of payments and the exchange rate?

INTRODUCTION

The exchange rate between one national currency and another is, like budget deficits and inflation, another economic variable which carries a heavy emotional charge. All too often it is regarded as the embodiment of national status and prestige. As in some well-known historical instances, the result is that outcomes in the *real* economy, such as output and employment, are frequently sacrificed in the pursuit of some arbitrary exchange rate target. Rather than making a fetish over the value of the exchange rate, common sense would seem to dictate that the best exchange rate policy in an individual jurisdiction is one which simply pursues stable and sensible macroeconomic policies for the domestic economy, regardless of their short-run impact on the exchanges.[1] In the long-run, after all, a healthy domestic economy is the best guarantee that the national currency will seem valuable to others. Yet in spite of the lessons of history, the conventional wisdom today seems to be not dissimilar to that prevailing around the time of the failed return to the gold standard in 1925. Arguments are frequently heard that the ideal international monetary system to promote world trade is a return to some form of fixed exchange rates, combined with a commitment to low or zero inflation on the part of the major player or players.

For all but two or three of the world's most powerful economies, any attempt to fix the exchange rate at some predetermined value involves giving up the ability to make crucial economic decisions (particularly monetary policy decisions) at the domestic level, and in essence tying the nation's economic fate entirely to that of its strongest trading partner. If, for example, there is an increase in foreign interest rates, even for reasons which have nothing to do with the domestic economy, then in order to maintain the exchange rate, interest rates at home must be raised also, regardless of whether or not this is appropriate in domestic conditions.

Giving up the ability to make domestic economic policy might conceivably be justified if the strongest foreign players could always be relied upon to pursue the best interests of the international community, rather than their own selfish concerns, but obviously there is no guarantee of this. More importantly, if the key economic decisions are made elsewhere this eliminates any genuine democratic scrutiny or control over the fate of the economy. As it is, contemporary central banks already lack political accountability and are dangerously remote from those whom their policies directly affect. The disenfranchisement of the domestic electorate is complete when all the relevant decisions are made by a foreign central bank or an international agency. The proposal for an eventual common currency in the European Union (EU) represents an extreme contemporary example of this process. In this case, power would shift entirely from national governments and electorates to a small elite of financial bureaucrats at the European central bank.

Current attitudes to exchange rate policy are possibly coloured by the recollection of the last period in which a worldwide regime of 'quasi-fixed' exchange rates was in place, the era of the Bretton Woods system from 1944–71. As discussed in chapter 2, in hindsight this was a period of remarkable economic prosperity. However, this should not be attributed to the exchange rate system itself, but to the fact that the major player, the USA, did pursue (whether by luck or design) financial policies which had the effect of maintaining an adequate level of world aggregate demand and hence world economic prosperity. In short, and possibly inadvertently, US administrations pursued the type of economic policies which are now so much derided by orthodox economic opinion. As soon as US policy began to go off the rails, however, specifically over the financing of the Vietnam War in the late 1960s, the Bretton Woods system fell apart.

In contrast to the Bretton Woods era, the period of the 'managed' or 'dirty' float from 1971–73 to the present has obviously been a time of increased economic instability. The ancient 'business cycle' of boom and bust, which had been thought to be tamed or even eliminated in the immediate postwar decades, has returned with full force. Again, however, as should be clear from the earlier discussion, the blame for this lies not with the exchange rate regime *per se*, but with the erratic and irresponsible macroeconomic policies pursued by the monetary and fiscal authorities in many jurisdictions. The major economic downturns of both the early 1980s and early 1990s were deliberately induced by the policy actions of key central banks worldwide in driving up real interest rates in the course of over-zealous campaigns against inflation. In current circumstances, if any individual nation were to take the courageous decision of trying to break free from this depressing cycle, it must be allowed some freedom of manoeuvre in exchange rate policy.

BALANCE OF PAYMENTS AND EXCHANGE RATE RELATIONSHIPS

The balance of payments is the statistical record of the domestic country's economic relationship with the rest of the world, expressed in terms of its own currency over some convenient accounting period such as a quarter or a year. Some straightforward manipulation of standard national income accounting relationships, as is done in every intermediate level textbook, reveals the following familiar relation between the main national accounts categories and the current account of the balance of payments. This is to be understood as an accounting identity rather than a matter of economic theory, and is therefore true by definition:

Government budget deficit + (Domestic investment – Domestic savings)
= Current account deficit

This expression is often interpreted as showing that if domestic savings are not enough to finance *both* domestic investment and the government budget deficit, the result must be a deficit on the current account of the balance of payments.

Its real economic significance may be better understood, however, with reference to another accounting identity, this time relating to a simple break-down of the balance of payments:

Current account + Capital account
= Changes in official holdings of foreign exchange reserves

In this second expression, the current account of the balance of payments should be taken to consist basically of exports less imports of goods and services, plus the net flow of income (interest and dividends) from foreign investments made in the past. The capital account refers to the net flows of *new* international borrowing and lending and equity investment. The usual way of looking at this is that if a nation has a current account deficit, meaning that it is not exporting enough to pay for imports plus interest and dividend payments due to foreigners, it must be borrowing from abroad to make up the difference. Therefore the capital account will be positive. The only alternative would be that the current account deficit is 'paid for' by the sale of official holdings of foreign currency assets (foreign exchange reserves). This source of financing, however, is obviously limited by the original size of the reserves. In the opposite case, when a nation has a current account surplus, it might be thought of as 'earning' funds which can then be invested abroad (implying capital outflow, or a negative capital account) or accumulated in the 'vaults' of the central bank in the form of additions to the foreign exchange reserves.

Although useful to explain the process in easy-to-understand terms, it should be stressed, nonetheless, that this view of a nation either earning, or not earning, its 'keep' and then being either rewarded or penalized by the change in its foreign credit position has probably never been factually accurate. It is certainly not accurate in the modern era of the global capital market. In practice, the direction of causality is very much the other way round. Because of the globalization of capital markets and the sheer speed, size and dominance of capital flows in the modern world, capital account developments come *first*, causing a subsequent reaction in the current account. A nation finding itself with a capital account surplus, in other words, must expect that the economy will somehow adjust so that it finds itself with a current account deficit also. The mechanism by which these adjustments occur is changes in the exchange rate. Needless to say, it is ultimately the real exchange rate, that is the relative price of goods and services in two jurisdictions expressed in a common currency, which is important for economic decision-making, as opposed to the nominal exchange rate, which is just the price of one currency expressed in terms of the other. It will be noted that the monetary policy (interest rate policy) of the domestic central bank, relative to what is going on elsewhere, is once again the key issue. When the central bank is pursuing a tight money policy to cure inflation, and hence driving up real interest rates relative to what is occurring elsewhere, this will lead to capital inflow. It will now be highly profitable to foreigners to lend to that jurisdiction. The increased real demand for domestic currency assets will then lead to a real exchange rate appreciation. The currency will be 'strong', which may be good for national prestige, but it will be a disaster for the nation's exporters who suddenly find that their wares now seem much more expensive from the point of view of foreigners, and they will not be able to sell them. In other words, domestic goods are now 'uncompetitive'. In this way, the current account deficit, whose appearance is, in any event, dictated by the algebra of the accounting identities, will be made a reality. This is in addition to the problems caused by the high interest rates in the first place.

The mechanism is, of course, similar to that envisaged in the orthodox description of open-economy crowding-out, but the difference is in how the initial change in interest rates is supposed to come about. If fiscal policy has little influence on the domestic rate of interest, as discussed in the previous chapter, then crowding-out is something of a misnomer. The process is more in the nature of a self-inflicted wound brought about by the high interest rate policy. There has been fierce debate about this issue in the classic case of the US 'twin deficits' of the early to mid-1980s. President Reagan's budget deficits were indeed associated with large deficits on the current account of the balance of payments (Marston, 1988; Smithin, 1990) just as the first accounting expression above would predict. However, main impetus for the high interest rates of the early 1980s, which set in train a sequence of events similar to that described above, came about *before* the deficits occurred. It must be attributed primarily to the dramatic change in the monetary policy regime described in previous chapters.

The domestic industrialists 'on the ground' will no doubt be bemused by their lack of success in foreign markets, in spite of having dutifully put into practice everything they had learned about increasing productivity in business school. In a real sense, of course, the failure is not theirs, but that of the policymakers, and ultimately those responsible for the economic theories by which policy is conducted. In any event, no amount of managerial effort, and none of the panaceas offered by the latest management 'gurus', will be of any help as long as the real exchange rate remains overvalued.

ALTERNATIVE EXCHANGE RATE REGIMES

At the textbook level, the debate about the appropriate international relationship between the competing national currencies has usually revolved around the issue of whether rates of exchange between the alternative standards of value should be 'floating' or 'fixed'. In the floating or flexible rate case, the exchange rate between any two national currencies is determined by the relative supplies and demands of the two currencies on the international financial markets. In the fixed rate case, the relationship between national currencies is kept within narrow limits, according to some international agreement or convention. Domestic central banks stand ready to take whatever action is necessary to force the value of the currency to remain within pre-set bounds. This would include intervention in the foreign exchange markets to buy or sell large volumes of the currency as required, and also changes in interest rates.

As well as the extremes of fixed and floating rates, there have also been advocates of some sort of compromise between the two in the form of a 'managed' or 'dirty' float. This is a situation where exchange rates are floating in principle, but the monetary authorities do take a view about what the appropriate exchange rate should be against one or all of its competitors at any point in time, and periodically take action to achieve this. Frequently also, some view is taken about the correct speed of appreciation or depreciation of the currency, if not the absolute level.

Another point of view, which has come very much to the fore in recent years, would be to push the concept of a fixed exchange rate to its logical conclusion and question whether there is any merit in the different jurisdictions having a separate currency at all. In other words, there are many who would advocate a 'single currency' or a 'currency union'. The effect of this would be to convert the many economies into a single economy, from the monetary point of view. Even if there are probably very few advocates of a single world currency at this point in time, the idea has been taken very seriously in the narrower context of the EU. Political developments of the late 1980s and early 1990s have led to ambitious (even overambitious) plans for a single currency in Europe, as embodied in the recommendations of the Delors Report of 1989 and the provisions of the Maastricht Treaty of 1991 (Delors, 1990; Kenen, 1992; Eichengreen, 1993).

The discussion in chapter 2 above illustrated how all of these concepts have been relevant over the course of the actual evolution of the international monetary system. The era of the international gold standard, from *c.* 1870 to 1914, was an era of a *de facto* fixed exchange rate system, and an extraordinarily rigid one at that. In contrast, the interwar period from 1918 to 1939 can only be described as an era of monetary disorder, with periods of floating rates, the failed attempts to restore the gold standard, and, as the world economy began to unravel, an aggressive regime of 'competitive depreciations' and 'beggar-thy-neighbour' trade policies. The Bretton Woods system, of 1944 to *c.* 1973, then restored a fixed exchange rate regime, but in a very much less rigid form than the old gold standard. Exchange rates were 'fixed but adjustable'. Finally, in the non-system that has been in place since around 1973, the major currencies, the most important of which now are the D-Mark, the yen and the US dollar, have been floating against one another. The present situation would probably be most correctly described as a managed or dirty float. This state of affairs has never seemed all that satisfactory to those involved, however, and there have been numerous proposals for reform, including a return to some sort of fixed exchange rate regime. Also, as mentioned, there have been attempts to create regional fixed rate regimes, as in the exchange rate mechanism (ERM) in Europe down to 1992/93, and the common currency proposal itself.

COVERED AND UNCOVERED INTEREST PARITY

The most salient feature of fixed exchange rate regimes, from the point of view of general economic prosperity, is that the monetary authorities in the small or medium-sized economies in such a system will lose whatever ability they previously had to influence the level of interest rates in their own jurisdictions. Monetary policy will be dictated by the major player or players. This may well therefore seem like a very destructive step to take, but none the less there have always been passionate advocates of fixed rate regimes throughout economic history, up to and including our own time. One thing in its favour is the apparently firmly entrenched belief that fixed exchange rates are necessary to promote and facilitate trade. There is, however, little or no factual evidence to back up this claim, as a number of economists including Feldstein (1992), Eichengreen (1993), and Smithin and Wolf (1993) have pointed out. More importantly, the debate over exchange rate regimes is also highly relevant to the struggle over who gains, and who loses, from the implementation of different monetary policy stances, as previously discussed in chapter 5. The key issue is whether or not the central bank of the 'hegonomic' power in the system is perceived to place a higher priority on fighting inflation and price stability than the other national central banks in the system. If so, a commitment to maintain a fixed exchange rate may recommend itself as a way of importing this style of monetary policy into the other jurisdictions, and effectively circumventing the domestic political constraints which might otherwise exist. Whatever impact this might have on the individual national economies, the position can always be defended by pointing to the technical requirements of maintaining the existing parity, the need for the nation to demonstrate 'commitment' to its partners, and simple national prestige.[2] In terms of the economic interest groups identified in earlier chapters, the more prosaic reality is that local financial élites in each nation are more inclined to trust the central bank of the hegonomic player in pursuing policies perceived to be in their own interest. Membership of the fixed exchange rate system suggests itself as a way to tie the hands of the local authorities, who might otherwise be more easily subject to domestic political pressures from the other interest groups. Obviously it is not too far-fetched to view the role of the German Bundesbank within the ERM in precisely this light. Of course, fixed exchange rate regimes need not inevitably be deflationary, given a different set of policies on the part of the key currency nation. The Bretton Woods system, for example, went in the other direction, and for that reason was unpopular with monetarists at the time (Smithin, 1991).

The relationship between interest rates and exchange rates is best understood by first considering the so-called 'covered interest parity' relationship in international finance. This condition states that the interest rate spread between domestic and foreign assets with similar intrinsic risk characteristics and terms to maturity, should be equal to the forward discount or premium on the exchange rate. In a world of 'perfect capital mobility', in which there are no technical, legal, or political barriers to the free movement of capital, this condition should hold. Rates of return must then be equal in all financial centres when expressed in a common currency (hedged by a forward contract). The implication is that the domestic interest rate can only be lower than foreign interest rates if the forward exchange rate, defined as the domestic currency price of one unit of foreign exchange for forward delivery, is also lower than the spot rate, i.e., the rate currently prevailing. In other words, as far as the players in the forward market are concerned, the domestic currency is expected to appreciate. This is not inconsistent with the more familiar idea that lowering interest rates will lead to a depreciation of the currency, because this refers to the impact on the spot rate, whereas the former statement refers to the forward rate. One way of interpreting the relationship is that a lower interest rate *now* will indeed depreciate the currency in spot terms, but that the market also typically expects the situation to return to 'normal' at some point in the future.

The usual argument these days would be that as the international capital market has become progressively more efficient and more liberal during the era of rapid technical change and 'globalization', the covered interest parity condition is more and more likely to hold in reality. Therefore, that differential interest rate movements between jurisdictions will be constrained to that extent. This does not necessarily mean, however, that there is no scope at all for an independent interest rate policy.

Even in a world in which perfect capital mobility (in a technical sense) is a reality, it is unlikely that the more stringent condition of 'perfect asset substitutability' will hold, as long as exchange rates are still free to change (Frankel, 1992). It remains unlikely that investors will treat assets denominated in different currencies as perfect substitutes for one another, even if their intrinsic risk characteristics are similar, as long as there is still some 'currency risk'. Therefore the spread between domestic and foreign interest rates need not be equal to the *actual* expected rate of depreciation or appreciation of the currency (as opposed to the forward premium or discount). The implication is obviously that the forward premium or discount is not precisely the same as the expected rate of depreciation or appreciation of the currency. They will differ by a 'risk premium' (or discount) which reflects the premium on the rate of interest required by foreign investors to acquire (uncovered) assets denominated in the domestic currency. In other words, it is not likely that 'uncovered interest parity' as opposed to 'covered interest parity' will hold, even if there is perfect capital mobility.

The scope for domestic interest rates to differ from those prevailing elsewhere, therefore, rests on the fact that exchange rates can change and are expected to change, and on the existence of the risk premium. The latter, in turn, exists because of the potential variability of exchange rates. Note that we can make much the same statement in this respect about real interest rates as can be made about nominal rates (Smithin, 1994a). The real interest rate spread between two jurisdictions depends on the expected real depreciation or appreciation of the exchange rate, plus the risk premium.

It follows that the act of joining a fixed exchange rate system (and *a fortiori*, for obvious reasons, a common currency area) will effectively restrict the scope for the domestic interest rate to deviate from foreign or 'world' rates. In a credible fixed exchange rate system, the exchange rate will not be expected to change (expected appreciation or depreciation will be zero) and there will be no risk premium. Therefore, domestic nominal interest rates will be equal to foreign interest rates, *unless* there are some actual impediments to capital mobility such as capital controls. As inflation rates will also converge in a fixed exchange rate regime, real interest rates will similarly converge. As mentioned, this will be perceived as a desirable thing by those groups who, for whatever reason, prefer the interest rate regime prevailing in the outside world to the regime that would likely be delivered by the domestic central bank operating independently.

THE GLOBALIZATION OF FINANCIAL MARKETS

In spite of the considerations discussed above, it has become more or less a staple of both the popular and financial press to argue that it is now almost completely anachronistic for the domestic monetary authorities to attempt to influence events in their own jurisdiction. In the modern world, it is said, they are more or less at the mercy of capricious worldwide economic trends, leaving them with no choice but to conform to whatever international market forces dictate, however unpalatable may be some of the actions which they are then 'forced' to take. This is rather vaguely supported by a sense that structural changes in the world economy at the end of the twentieth century, the much discussed but disparate developments which are often lumped together under the heading of 'globalization',[3] make the very idea of exchange rate flexibility, independent national currencies, and potential 'cheap money' policies, somehow obsolete and unviable. In this type of argument, particular stress is laid on contemporary technological and regulatory changes in financial markets which have vastly increased and facilitated international capital movements. According to some proponents, these trends have effectively established a 'global capital market' which supposedly undermines any attempts by individual jurisdictions at an independent policy. It is not usually made clear just who does set monetary policy and interest rates in this framework, other than worldwide market forces.

We have seen, however, that this argument is essentially spurious. What the globalization of financial markets actually does is to move the world closer and closer to a situation of technical perfect capital mobility, as defined earlier. In other words, it means that the condition of covered interest parity will be more and more likely to hold. As long as there are separate currencies and exchange rates are free to move, however, the technical changes *per se* are unlikely to increase the scope for perfect asset substitutability. But, it is the latter that would be required for the domestic authorities to legitimately claim that they have 'no choice', whenever interest rates are raised. Much more frequently such episodes are quite literally a matter of choice, the alternative being simply to let the exchange rate depreciate.

The real result of the increased international mobility in recent years, is actually to dramatically reinforce the point made above, that capital account developments dominate the current account and that the trade performance of a nation emerges as little more than a side-effect of what is happening in the international capital markets. This may be an undesirable and uncomfortable development for all sorts of reasons, but it is not at all clear that it points to the conclusion that national economic policymakers should respond by giving up whatever leverage over monetary policy they still do possess. The scenario outlined here may actually imply that monetary policy becomes even *more* significant. As discussed, under contemporary conditions an increase in domestic real interest rates very rapidly causes capital inflow and real currency appreciation, doing even greater damage to the export and import-competing industries, over and above that caused by the rise in interest rates in the first place. This, however, seems to be rather an argument for giving very careful thought about what a sensible monetary policy might be, in the new environment, than for abandoning control of the remaining monetary levers either to the central bank of some other nation, or to an international bureaucracy.

THE LESSONS OF RECENT HISTORY

Events in Europe over the past few years, involving the near-collapse of the ERM of the European Monetary System (EMS), do in fact provide a classic illustration of the problems which arise when an obsessive concern with exchange rate policy takes precedence over the real economy. The experience of Britain, during and after that country's short-lived membership of the ERM in 1990–92, as discussed earlier in chapter 2, is particularly instructive. Apart from the desire to show Britain's willingness to support the movement towards greater European unity, for British financial or 'rentier' interests, the theory was that the Bundesbank was traditionally tougher on inflation than the Bank of England was likely to be. Hence, by limiting the fluctuations of the pound against the D-Mark, the hope was that stringent German anti-inflation policy would be imported to Britain.

The results of this reasoning were disastrous in practice, and Britain was plunged into a severe recession in the 1991–92 period. Maintaining the exchange value of the pound against the D-Mark required punishingly high interest rates, particularly at a time when the Bundesbank was continuously tightening monetary policy (raising interest rates) in an effort to reduce the inflationary pressures arising from the costs of German unification. Under the strain of high real rates of interest there was no chance for Britain's economy to recover, and maintaining a high value of the pound against the D-Mark and other European currencies was counter-productive from the point of view of stimulating exports.

Eventually Britain was forced to leave the ERM after the exchange rate crisis of September 1992. This was a blow to the international prestige of the government, but from the economic point of view the crisis provided much-needed relief from deflationary pressure. The authorities were now free to lower interest rates and the pound was allowed to depreciate against the D-Mark and other currencies, making British exports more competitive. The economy immediately began to recover and over the next year the British economy was alone among the major EU economies in having positive economic growth. Also, contrary to the alarmist views expressed in some quarters at the time, the pound did not go into a free-fall and was actually beginning to rise again in value by the following summer.

In the case of Britain, the saving grace of the more recent debacle may be that the current generation has now had the opportunity to relearn the same hard lessons about exchange rate policy as did their forebears at the time of the failed return to the gold standard more than 60 years ago. Hopefully, policymakers in other countries could also try to profit from this experience. The basic lesson to learn is surely that monetary and fiscal policy decisions, and, in particular, central bank policy over interest rates, should be dominated by what is best for domestic output and employment and not by their immediate impact on the exchange rate. A depressingly frequent justification for interest rate increases, even in a depressed economy, is to 'protect the value of the currency'. In the end, however, only a prosperous and thriving economy is truly able to achieve this.

THE SCOPE FOR MONETARY SOVEREIGNTY

Paraskevopoulos, Paschakis and Smithin (forthcoming) have shown that, theoretically, a mechanism does exist whereby the small or 'medium-sized' open economy can achieve monetary sovereignty even in modern conditions. This rests on the important distinction between 'capital flight' and capital outflow, and on the beneficial impact an increase in a nation's foreign credit position is likely to have on the risk premium. If such a nation does succeed in depressing real interest rates to lower levels than those prevailing elsewhere then there is no question that, in equilibrium, the end result is both a permanent real depreciation of the currency and an increase in the real net foreign credit position.

However, is it *not* the case that this process is necessarily unstable, which seems to be the implicit assumption of those who fear that any decrease in interest rates will immediately panic the semi-mythical 'international bond-holders'. The conclusion holds even in the modern environment with essentially no barriers to capital mobility, except the basic condition that promises-to-pay denominated in different currencies are not perfect substitutes. The increase in the foreign credit position may actually have a beneficial impact on the risk premium demanded by foreign investors to hold assets denominated in the domestic currency (Branson, 1988) and this enables the gap between foreign and domestic real interest rates to be maintained.

Although lower domestic real interest rates do lead to capital outflow and a real depreciation of the currency, just as the usual arguments suggest, the point is that this is not necessarily a bad thing from the perspective of the 'credit rating' of the domestic economy. First, the current account will improve. Second, it should be recalled that another name for capital outflow, after all, is foreign investment. If this does not become actual capital flight, in which both the capitalists and their funds decamp, a domestic country experiencing capital outflow is actually building up a net credit position with the rest of the world which will generate a future flow of interest and dividend income to domestic residents. To the extent that the promises to pay of creditor nations are regarded as more trustworthy and reliable than those of debtor nations, which is usually assumed to be the case, this may improve the international status of the currency rather than damage it. If low real interest rates are also good for output and employment, as has been suggested above, there may well therefore be a 'virtuous cycle' in nations with low but still positive real rates of interest.

CONCLUSION

If, as suggested above, the conduct of monetary policy, and specifically control over interest rates, is one of the most important determinants of real economic outcomes such as the level of output and employment, then it follows that even in the contemporary 'global economy' those national economic authorities which retain political accountability for the economic well-being of their citizens would be well advised to maintain domestic control over monetary policy in so far as this is possible. This cannot be done if priority is given to exchange rate and balance of payments issues, and is voluntarily abdicated when a small open economy joins a fixed exchange rate regime or common currency area.

There is, of course, no guarantee that the performance of the national monetary authority would always be an improvement upon that of either a supranational central bank in a currency union, or the leading player (key currency nation) of a fixed exchange rate system. After all, the drastic world-wide shift in monetary policy occurring at the end of the 1970s and early 1980s, which we are calling the 'Revenge of the Rentiers', occurred in the context of the post-Bretton Woods 'managed' or 'dirty' float. It was essentially a question of *all* central banks being subject to similar political pressures, and ideological and theoretical currents, at more or less the same time. However, the retention of separate national currencies, which either float or are at least subject to periodic revaluations, does at least allow for a *potential* escape route from the strait-jacket that centralized monetary policy could become. Even if, in practice, individual national central banks have sometimes pursued more draconian policies than the international average (the recent record of the Bank of Canada, as compared to the US Fed, is a good example) there is at least some hope that a national rather than supranational central bank may be eventually more responsive to the political will of those directly affected by their policies.

This seems to be a crucially important consideration at the current juncture in history (Smithin, 1995a). Although it is often suggested that one of the *advantages* of a supranational institution is that it is more removed from the political process (and, hence, in the current climate, freer to impose a *deflationary* bias to its policies), the opposite point of view is surely more defensible on the grounds of basic democratic principles.

Note that to suggest that individual national jurisdiction should retain some freedom of manoeuvre over exchange rates is not to advocate wildly fluctuating exchange rates or an unstable international financial system *per se*. As pointed out in Chapter 2 the causality is the other way round in this case. If all nations could simultaneously be persuaded to pursue stable and sensible policies promoting full employment, but to avoid the excessive inflationary consequences of the negative real interest rates of the 1970s, then the result would simply be world-wide prosperity *and* stable exchange rates and an orderly international financial system. On the other hand, if one or more major nations continues to pursue the destructive type of policies witnessed in the last twenty years, then there can be no hope of a stable international financial system, regardless of the formal characteristics of the exchange rate regime. The best that an individual jurisdiction can hope for in these circumstances is 'sauve qui peut'. There is no point in tying the domestic currency to an international standard which is unstable anyway.

NOTES

1. It is true that this will provide no defence against an impact on the exchanges caused by bad policies on the part of the nation's trading partners, but in any event there is presumably little that can be done about economic policy in foreign countries, except continued efforts at education and persuasion at the international level.
2. Consider, for example, the concept of the 'franc fort' (strong franc) in late twentieth century French politics.
3. See 'Fear of finance: a survey of the world economy', *The Economist*, 19 September 1992.

8. Macroeconomics and the stock market

INTRODUCTION

One of the basic ideas of financial and economic commentary is that there is a definite link between the type of macroeconomic events and policies discussed in this book and the behaviour of the stock market. For example, the notion that the famous stock market crash of 1929 was actually the *cause* of the Great Depression of the 1930s is a widely-held view among financial commentators and the general public, as well as some professional economists (Galbraith, 1954; 1979, 1994). A possibly more sensible view is (again) that the direction of causality goes the other way around, that the ups and downs of the business cycle are themselves responsible for the ups and downs of the stock market. For example, consider the following quotation from a guide to potential investors put out by a Toronto publishing house in the 1980s:[1]

> The rise and fall of the stock market generally reflects a complex series of cause and effect relationships among various sectors of the economy, as well as among different stock groups. The beginning of a business cycle is usually the beginning of a rising stock market (also called a 'bull market'). At this time investors tend to show a lingering preference for big name or blue-chip stocks. With interest rates low, consumers start to buy cars and household goods, so the stocks of consumer product companies begin to rise. As demand continues to grow consumer product companies look to expand their manufacturing capacity. Banks are then called upon to provide the necessary financing, so their business grows. Unemployment falls. Orders increase for raw materials and industrial stocks begin to rise.
>
> All this economic growth leads to a more buoyant stock market. And with the market's increased momentum, investors are more confident. As dwindling supplies of raw materials push commodity and metal prices upward, investors become more willing to buy the riskier stocks of resource companies such as mining, oil and gas, and real estate companies. During a rising business cycle there is usually a bull market. But now inflation begins to push up interest rates, and inevitably, the time of reckoning comes. Higher interest rates signal the start of the falling business cycle, and probably a 'bear' (or falling) market, which continues until the economy picks up and the stock market starts to rise again.

This is actually quite a reasonable description of the process, except that it has interest rates rising as a result of mysterious 'market forces' rather than explicit decisions by those in charge of monetary policy, and it also does not take into account a strange phenomenon of more recent years, which is that now the stock market sometimes *falls* when the economic news is apparently good. To take a small example, on one day in December 1994 the Canadian financial press reported a rough time on the stock market the previous day, but noted that the only economic news that had been reported was quite positive. For example, it was reported that US real GDP growth in the third quarter was greater than expected, up to 3.9 per cent at an annualized rate, from 3.4 per cent, and that the Chicago Purchasing Management Association index was up by 3.1 percentage points in November.[2] This type of thing (the stock market falling on 'good' news) has been happening quite frequently in recent years. Presumably the market players have intuitively figured out the likely sequence of events that has been described in this book, the new rules of the game since the late 1970s, and are several steps ahead. If the economy is doing well, this will likely lead to a resurgence of inflation. Given that inflation is now the main concern of central banks, they will inevitably respond with higher real interest rates to beat inflation back down again. The high real interest rates will then slow down the economy and reduce profitability. Thus, by a perverse logic, good news is actually bad news and the market responds accordingly. In a similar vein, McQuaig (1995: 152–3) quotes from a financial newsletter which refers to the 'spectre of full employment', an interesting concept to say the least.

The purpose of this chapter is to investigate the links between the stock market and the macroeconomy in more detail. The method chosen to do this is to look at two concrete examples, the famous stock market 'crashes' of 1929, and, more recently, 1987. One important issue to consider is why, if the 1929 crash supposedly had such dire consequences, the 1987 episode apparently passed off so much more easily. The general conclusion which emerges is that market players do seem to instinctively understand the economic mechanisms that have been discussed in this book. The different course of events as between the two episodes provides considerable support for the arguments that have been put forward, and in particular the problems caused by the deliberate manipulation of interest rates in the effort to cure inflation.

THE STOCK MARKET CRASHES OF 1987 AND 1929

The stock market crash of October 1987 was one of the most dramatic economic events of the 1980s, if not necessarily the most important. It brought to an end in a spectacular fashion the great bull market of the 1980s, which had begun five years earlier in 1982.

The crash was a worldwide phenomenon. In New York on Monday, 19 October the Dow Jones index of the New York Stock Exchange lost 508 points in a single day or 22.6 per cent of its value. At the close of trading on 19 October, the index was off 36 per cent from the peak of the bull market in August. In other centres, the FT index in London was off 22 per cent in the two days of 19 and 20 October, the Nikkei index in Tokyo fell by 15 per cent on 20 October (the largest one-day fall in 35 years), and the TSE 300 in Toronto lost 408 points, or 11 per cent of its value, on the 19th.[3]

Naturally comparisons were made to the other great stock market crash of 1929. In fact, the magnitude of the fall on Wall Street on 19 October 1987 was actually greater than that of 'Black Tuesday' on 29 October 1929 when the market was off by 'only' 11.7 per cent. The difference is that the stock market slide of the late 1920s and early 1930s was not confined to a single day. Although the particularly dramatic episodes will always be remembered, the collapse of stock market values (interspersed by temporary rallies and revivals) eventually went on for a number of years. At the depth of the Great Depression in 1933 the stock market had lost 80 per cent of its value at the pre-crash peak. In the immediate aftershock of 1987, however, the comparisons with 1929 were inevitable, and naturally led to a great deal of public anxiety about the economic future.

Part of the deeply ingrained popular folklore about the course of the Great Depression of the 1930s is that the 1929 crash was somehow a direct cause of the collapse of real economic activity, as opposed to a symptom or side-effect of it.[4] It is not surprising, therefore, that in the aftermath of the October 1987 crash there were widespread fears that history was about to repeat itself. The idea that the 1929 crash led directly to the Depression has not been the conventional view among academic economists (with some influential exceptions, as noted), but, in the event, whatever fears of gloom and doom the public may have been harbouring were amply reinforced in October and November 1987 by an outpouring of commentary by professional economic forecasters and market analysts, to the effect that a serious recession was now inevitable and was just around the corner.[5]

A NON-EVENT?

In spite of the panic-stricken forecasts of October and November, however, no catastrophe of the scale of the 1930s (or even of the early 1980s) appeared on the immediate horizon. As time passed during 1988, fears of a recession directly caused by the stock market crash simply evaporated. In April and October 1988, the financial and popular press in many of the countries affected published 'six months after' and 'one year after' retrospectives. Now, the tone of the commentary was how little had changed, how robust economic growth had been, and how fears of recession had been exaggerated.[6]

The crash of 1987 was in danger of being remembered as the great non-event of economic history, except presumably by those who actually lost large sums of money. As an illustration of how much attitudes had changed, by September 1988 *The Economist* magazine of London was actually able to state that: '(a)ll in all...the stockmarket crash did no great harm and probably did some good'.[7] This was on the dubious grounds that it helped to dampen the growth in aggregate demand in the USA (and hence helped to restrain inflation) and provided some incentive for Washington policymakers to take the problem of the US budget deficit more seriously. The atmosphere of the autumn of 1988, clearly, was a good deal different from that of the previous year. On 19 October 1988 the Dow Jones index in New York stood at 2137.27, marking a recovery of 398 points, and 23 per cent, from the close of 1738.41 one year earlier.

THE STOCK MARKET AND THE REAL ECONOMY

Even if the initial furore about the 1987 crash soon died down, several questions clearly remain to be answered about the links, if any, between this extraordinary episode in financial history and the course of events in the real world of macroeconomics and macroeconomic policy.

It is necessary to enquire, first, what were the causes of the crash of 1987, and whether they were in any way related to the events in the world macroeconomy of the 1980s. Second, whether there is any logic at all in the view, apart from dubious analogies to 1929, that the crash itself might have led to a recession or depression. Third, if there is any logic in that view, why did the advertised recession not emerge through 1988?

There was, of course, another world recession in the 1990–91 period, as discussed earlier. But, it is obvious that this occurred as a result of events and policy decisions which occurred well after the 1987 crash, specifically in 1989 (after the US presidential elections of 1988), and in the following years. There was no direct connection to the 1987 episode.

CAUSES OF THE 1987 CRASH?

Commentary on the causes of the 1987 crash seems to fall into three broad categories. One view is that it was simply the verdict of 'the markets' on the fiscal policy of the Reagan administration, and in particular on the existence of the 'twin deficits', the budget deficit and trade deficit, as discussed in chapter 7 above. The fact that the financial panic was a worldwide affair would not damage this view, given the importance of US developments for the rest of the world economy. Among those who had been critical of US fiscal and exchange rate policies, the immediate reaction was that the crash was something of a day of reckoning for 'Reaganomics'. Certainly, some elements of the situation lent superficial support for this type of view. Among the items of news which the markets had received in the days immediately before the crash had been an announcement on 14 October (the previous Wednesday) that the unadjusted monthly trade figures for August had been worse than expected at $15.5 billion. Attention also focused on some ill-timed remarks by the US Treasury Secretary James Baker, in the context of a dispute over monetary policy with West Germany, to the effect that the Americans were prepared to allow the value of the US dollar to fall still further than it already had done.[8]

In keeping with the view that the markets were unhappy about the twin deficits, there was indeed a flurry of activity in the weeks after the crash to do something about the budget deficit (and hence the trade deficit). This resulted in a 'summit' between the President and the Congress which agreed on a package of budget cuts on 20 November. The package of cuts, however, was regarded by most commentators as derisory, and, in any event, the US budget deficit was already lower as a percentage of GDP than it had been a couple of years earlier. These observations cast considerable doubt on the idea that fiscal policy and the twin deficits were really at the root of the trouble. If so, and the markets have any degree of rationality at all, why had the crash not come two years earlier in 1985?

The factor which finally dispelled the idea that the 1987 crash was Ronald Reagan's economic Waterloo over the budget and trade deficits, was simply the lack of further excitement either in the markets or the real economy through 1988. The budget and trade deficits persisted through 1988 on the course that had seemed to be established in 1987 (a gradual reduction of both as a proportion of GDP but with no spectacular changes) and certainly both deficits excited much less comment in the media than in the previous two years. The value of the US dollar did fall after the crash, and in early 1988, but then recovered later in the year. As there was simply a slow evolution of the pre-existing situation through 1988, it is hard to make the case, in retrospect, that the 1987 crash represented some decisive rejection by the markets of the administration's economic record up to that point. (This does not necessarily imply, of course, that the administration's record was good.)

A second view of the crash is that the last months of the bull market in 1987 were yet another example of a 'speculative bubble' in assets markets of which there have been many other cases in history, including the 1929 episode itself, the South Sea Bubble of early eighteenth-century England, and the tulip bulb mania of seventeenth-century Holland. During a speculative fever, rising prices are simply driven by the expectations of future rises, and, for a while, become self-fulfilling. The speculator is willing to pay a high price today on the assumption that somebody else will be prepared to pay an even higher price tomorrow. Prices can quickly become detached from anything which even remotely approximates the true economic value of the asset. According to professional stock market watchers, the evidence that pure speculation is taking hold is to be seen in ever increasing p/e (price/earnings) ratios, apparently defying the laws of gravity. The average p/e ratio on the New York stock exchange in October 1987 had reached a value of about 20 – high by historical standards.

At some point, clearly, if the asset prices have lost touch with the underlying fundamentals, and the process is kept going only by psychology, a speculative bubble will burst. At some stage, the confident expectation that prices will rise forever starts to flag and the market becomes jittery. All that is then needed is a spark for the tinderbox. It will dawn on the investors that the assets they have acquired are not really worth the price they have paid, and they will try to get rid of them while the going is good. Soon everyone is selling and there is a fully-fledged panic.

In 1987, it surely must have been the case that at least some psychological element was involved, even if this view is heresy to theoretical economists who are proponents of rational expectations and efficient markets. It is not really true, after all, that the events of October 1987 came entirely as a bolt from the blue, even if the magnitude of the drop was a shock. In fact, fears were expressed in the financial press and elsewhere *throughout the year* that stock markets all over the world were getting into a jittery state. The market was 'climbing a wall of fear' as the well-worn cliche would have it, indicating that the bull market had probably gone on for too long, but was still none the less rising. Investors were torn between getting out safely while the going was good, and staying in to squeeze the last drop of profit out of the still rising market. It is easy to see that a market in this state would be ultimately subject to a dramatic collapse of some kind, even if not necessarily of the proportions which did occur.

The noted economist, Lester Thurow, in a syndicated newspaper article, has made the point that the crash was simply the correction of a speculative bubble, in the following way[9]:

(c)rashes are rational market adjustments; what is irrational are the prices before the crash. What was true in tulip mania has been true in every crash since. The post-crash prices are seen as sane; the pre-crash prices as insane. The 1987 September price/earnings ratios were simply unsustainable. The October crash was rational.

One point in favour of this view is that, in retrospect, after the markets had bounced back somewhat in the last months of 1987, the effect of the crashes on Wall Street and in London was little more than to restore share values at the end of 1987 to what they had been at the start of the year. The October episode could therefore reasonably be seen as just wiping out the excessive speculative gains of the dying months of the bull.

A third approach to the causes of the stock market crash has been to downplay external factors and look for causes in the internal operations of the markets (as institutions) themselves. The argument, in other words, is that once a downturn in stock prices started (from whatever external cause), it was turned into a panic by weaknesses in the technical operations of the stock market itself. Comment along these lines in both the financial press and in official circles in the USA has focused on the technical and institutional features of contemporary equities markets, such as the growing importance of institutional investors (e.g. pension funds), the computerization of the trading process, and the relationship between the new markets in stock index futures and the underlying cash market. The combination of these developments lead to innovative trading strategies in the 1980s, including program trading, index arbitrage, and portfolio insurance, the operation of all of which, so some observers believe, can exacerbate a downturn and turn it into a panic. The efficiency of the specialist system of market-making on the New York stock exchange was also questioned.

The report of the 'President's Task Force on Market Mechanisms' in the USA, the so-called 'Brady Commission' was released only some two months after the crash, on 8 January 1988. It did, in fact, exclusively concentrate on these technical issues. A large part of the blame for the panic was placed on the computerized portfolio insurance strategies of a few large traders, whose automatic sell orders triggered by a market decline helped to make it worse. The recommendations of the report included such items as a need for so-called 'circuit breakers' (organized trading halts) during a time of crisis, the regulation of the interdependent cash, options, and futures markets, by a single agency, higher margins in futures markets, and the opening of the books of the market-makers (for information purposes) at a time of severe imbalance between buy and sell orders (Greenwald and Stein, 1988; Gammill and Marsh, 1988; Leland and Rubenstein, 1988).

The technical market mechanisms approach, however, rather too obviously misses the forest for the trees. As has been pointed out, there have been numerous examples of speculative bubbles and spectacular crashes both in equities markets and other assets markets throughout recorded history. These occurred long before there were any computers, and in diverse institutional contexts in which today's financial buzzwords would be meaningless. Similar crashes could also, quite predictably, occur again at some point in the future in similar economic circumstances, regardless of any reforms the present generation can make in response to yesterday's crisis. One can imagine similar exercises to the Brady Report having been undertaken, either formally or informally, after each of the historical episodes, and no matter how accurate and penetrating the hypothetical reports might have been on a technical level for their own time, they clearly would have had no way of foreseeing and regulating the mutations and permutations of the financial and equity markets of the present day. A similar fate would befall any purely technical changes in the structure of financial markets made today.

One point to note is that it has often been the process of a boom itself which has prompted clever financial innovations, so-called 'new wrinkles' for taking maximum advantage of it. These new techniques have always seemed foolproof, the invention of financial genius, during a rising market, but just as regularly they fall apart when the market starts to decline. Hence, if and when the time is ripe for a new speculative boom to occur, the markets can be relied upon to find a way for it to happen, whatever the current regulations. Then when panic sets in, a crash will also occur, unhindered by the rules imposed to prevent a repetition of the last crisis.

THE ROLE OF MONETARY POLICY

The one factor which has not so far been discussed as one of the possible causes of the 1987 stock market crash is in many ways the most plausible. This is that by the fall of 1987, after five years of economic expansion, and because of indications that the inflation rate was trending upwards once more, the markets had begun to fear a return to the tight money policies of the earlier 1980s, with high interest rates and recessionary conditions.

In spite of the often-repeated formula that a low inflation rate is a precondition of economic prosperity, the hard-bitten players in the world's stock markets realize instinctively, and from bitter experience, that it is actually the attempts to *achieve* low inflation that are disastrous for industrial production and business profits. Hence, in the context of 1987, any sign of a return to the conditions of the monetarist experiment of 1979–82 would certainly be bad for the stock market. In this sense, the crash may be seen as a verdict, not just on the contemporary fiscal and exchange rate policy of the Reagan administration, but on the entire philosophy of macroeconomic policymaking which characterized the 1980s, and for that matter is still with us today.

Obviously, the purely speculative and psychological considerations stressed above are important in explaining just how far stock prices will go in the later stages of a boom, and the timing and magnitude of the final bursting of the bubble. In the long-run, however, and without insisting on an exact correlation of the stock market and the real economy, the rise and fall of the stock market must be related to the underlying performance of the real economy. The real foundation for rising stock prices is ultimately the rising profitability of the firms whose ownership the stocks represent, which in turn (for the majority of firms) depends on the underlying prosperity of the macroeconomy.

The bull market of the 1980s, in fact, in North America and elsewhere, having begun in 1982, coincided quite precisely with the phase of recovery and renewed prosperity after the severe recessions of the first few years of the decade. The year 1982 marked the low point of the US recession, but before the year was out it was clear that the political consequences of high unemployment and falling output had provoked a temporary change in the course of monetary policy, after the monetarist experiment. As James Tobin (1985: 10) has put it: 'Paul Volcker and his colleagues [had] chose[n] the economy over M1, to universal relief'. Also, it should have been apparent that the Reagan tax cuts of the previous year would soon begin to have their effects on fiscal policy. Hence the stage was set for the US recovery, and, given the importance of the US economy, at least a partial recovery for other countries also. Thereafter, there was an unbroken expansion for five years until 1987, so the fact that the stock market was also rising during this period is not surprising. The fact that inflation also remained low for some time during the boom was a bonus, so that having started from a feeling of gloom and doom in 1982, the prevailing economic mood in the G7 as 1987 began was one of optimism.

The key change which occurred in 1987, however, was that the temporarily forgotten topic of inflation began to return to the agenda. After half-a-decade of growth without (much) inflation, and, in the USA, six years in which measured inflation had fallen every year, the inflation numbers began to turn upward once again. The increases were marginal and clearly rates of price increases were still nothing like the orders of magnitude of the late 1970s, but the reaction from those who regard inflation as the most important economic problem was predictable. There were immediate calls for a tighter money policy to 'nip inflation in the bud' and to cool down 'overheating' economies. The argument was that it was better to take action immediately and risk a (hopefully) brief economic slowdown now, rather than do nothing and allow the inflation rate to build up to the levels of seven or eight years earlier, at which point it might take a very serious recession to cure it. The atmosphere of the time was captured by a notable cover put out by the influential magazine *The Economist* on 1 August 1987. This bore the legend:

THE RETURN OF INFLATION: COMING SOON TO A COUNTRY NEAR YOU

Inflation was depicted as a green monster. The lead story made the point that inflation was rising again, and made a comparison between the then current situation and the inflationary booms of the early and late 1970s, both of which were brought to an end by serious recessions.

By this stage, of course, it was already difficult to discuss monetary policy in terms of traditional monetarism, because of the effect of financial innovation on the interpretation of the monetary aggregates. Hence, commentators and analysts now tended to infer the stance of monetary policy directly from the behaviour of real and nominal interest rates, in what had been (before the 1970s) the time-honoured fashion. In these terms it seemed clear, in the USA and elsewhere over the summer of 1987, that monetary policy was indeed tightening.

There were a number of symbolic incidents indicating the trend of monetary policy during that summer. On 4 September the new chairperson of the Fed, Alan Greenspan, who had replaced Paul Volcker less than a month before, raised the US discount rate to 6 per cent. Although the discount rate in itself may not be the most important tool of monetary policy, changes in the rate do have what monetary economists call an 'announcement effect'. This was the first increase since 1984, and would certainly give an indication of the intended course of things to come. There must originally have been some uncertainty in the marketplace about the future direction of monetary policy under the new chairperson. Hence, the fact that one of the first policy changes was an increase in the discount rate may have been interpreted as a sign that, like Mr Volcker eight years previously, the new chair would attempt to establish his credentials as a tough 'inflation fighter' at an early stage.

Also, in Britain, there had been a similar incident on 6 August when the authorities had induced a one percentage point rise in the base lending rates of the major banks. On that occasion, significantly, the London stock market lost 4 per cent of its value in two trading days on 6 and 7 August.[10]

As it was the apparent upturn in inflation which originally provoked these events, it should be stressed, once again, that in the conditions of the mid-1980s it was not so much a resurgence of inflation *per se* about which stock markets were concerned, but the authorities' possible reaction to it. The fear would be that the response would be an all-out deflation as earlier in the decade with high real interest rates, high unemployment and (most importantly from the shareholders' point of view) falling business profits. Even a remote possibility of a return to the conditions of the early 1980s, which were still fresh in the memory, would be a sufficient reason for the stock markets to become nervous. What is being suggested, therefore, is that it was this possibility of a return to the conditions of 1979–82 which explains not only the relatively minor stock market collapse in Britain in August, but also the later worldwide crash in October.

The monetary policy angle obviously does not explain why the crash occurred specifically on 19 October, rather than some other date. However, if the apparent shift in monetary policy made for a generally nervous atmosphere, then it would be at this point that the superficial events reported in the press, such as the unexpectedly bad trade figures for a single month, or the ill-considered remarks by US government officials, or one of any number of other news items, would take on an apparent significance that they would not have done under other circumstances. In the end, the search for the 'straw which broke the camel's back' is probably futile. With the markets uneasy over the trend of monetary policy, and given the speculative run-up of asset values that occurred in the dying stages of the bull market, it might be argued that the markets were primed for a fall (if not a crash) by October 1987, and that almost any item of apparently bad economic news would have been a good excuse to set off the panic.

WHAT BECAME OF THE RECESSION OF 1988?

In spite of the dire predictions of the winter of 1987/88, as the year 1988 wore on it began to seem to many financial commentators and analysts that the most significant thing about the stock market crash of 1987 was its *lack* of effect on the real economy. The reasons for this are also plausibly closely connected to the conduct of monetary policy.

A stock market crash could potentially affect the real economy through only two or three channels. The two that are usually stressed are a so-called 'wealth effect' on consumption spending, and the 'confidence' effect on the investment spending plans of the private sector.

As for the wealth effect, a reduction in asset values clearly does reduce the wealth of those who are affected, and to the extent that (a) the level of wealth affects consumption spending decisions, and (b) such demand-side changes affect real output and employment, the impact would be contractionary. The popular image of this has to do with the sudden change in the fortunes of stockbrokers and others involved in the financial services industry, but for this type of effect to have any real force it would have to refer not to the commission *incomes* of this limited number of people but to the wealth of their customers.

There are, in fact, also more general reasons for doubting the practical significance of the wealth effect, as the consumption spending of stock market participants is probably not the largest fraction of total consumption spending, and it is doubtful whether the consumption spending even of this segment of the population is mainly influenced by the value of their assets or wealth, rather than by other factors such as their current labour income. Also, in the case of the 1987 episode it must be remembered that the effect of the crash (after the markets had stabilized) was little more than to reduce the value of stocks at year-end 1987 to where they had been at the beginning of the year (already a high level), and it is hard to imagine that this in itself would be a cause of significant belt-tightening. None the less, fear that a wealth effect would reduce consumption spending was one of the factors behind the pessimistic forecasts immediately after the 1987 crash.

The confidence effect on private investment spending is the other potential channel by which a crash may transmit a negative impulse to the real economy. The general atmosphere of gloom and doom may induce firms to postpone investment expenditures which they had previously been planning, and this effect may be compounded by the lack of confidence on the part of prospective shareholders when a new issue is floated on the market. Even if firms remain sufficiently confident to undertake new projects, they may have difficulty raising the capital to finance them.

If, in spite of the doubts raised here about the quantitative significance of the wealth effect, it is feared that either or both of the wealth effect and the confidence effect are operative in a particular situation, then the usual argument would be that a quick response by the monetary authorities may be the only practical method of avoiding a recession. For largely institutional reasons (the length of time taken by the budget process), a fiscal policy response would be inadequate.

There are two aspects to the role of monetary policy in a genuine crisis. The first is a short-term technical issue. When a full-blown panic is underway, and asset valuations are rapidly falling, the immediate creditworthiness of the market participants is automatically called into question, even in cases where this would not be a problem on sober long-term reflection after the immediate crisis has passed (Greenwald and Stein, 1988). When any type of financial panic is in progress, therefore, the responsible monetary authorities must perform their 'lender of last resort' function, i.e. they must provide emergency liquidity to the market to prevent the unwarranted collapse of some of the main players, and hence a worsening of the crisis. This has been a key principle of central banking since the time of Bagehot (1873; 1915) and before.

The second point is that a continued expansionary monetary policy over a longer time horizon can offset either the wealth effect or the negative confidence effect, if these threaten to plunge the economy into a recession. To be sure, this would have been decried as 'fine-tuning' at the zenith of the policy irrelevance debates of the 1970s, but under the pressure of an actual crisis the academic arguments for doing nothing do tend to seem less convincing than usual.

In fact, most academic economists, and certainly the central banking community, are familiar with Milton Friedman's argument that in similar circumstances 60 years before, the Great Depression was caused not by the 1929 crash *per se*, but by a perverse response of the fledgling Federal Reserve

System to the crisis. According to Friedman, the Federal Reserve Bank of New York did at first make a move towards providing the required liquidity to the markets, but then more conservative forces at the Federal Reserve Board (in Washington) prevailed. Through 1930 and on to 1933, the money supply was actually allowed to decline, eventually by as much as one-third, prices fell, and real interest rates rose. This led inevitably to a banking crisis (exacerbated by the weaknesses of the US banking system at that time) and, via the familiar argument about the (short-run) effects of monetary policy on real output, to the Great Depression (Friedman and Friedman, 1980: 79–84). Friedman would argue that this episode reinforces the general case for a monetary rule (removing the power of the central bank to make *any* discretionary changes in monetary policy), but, when faced with a crisis in an environment in which the idealized rules have *not* been followed, the positions of Friedman and the believers in monetary management temporarily converge. Both would then accept that central bankers do have the power to avoid the worst consequences.

In 1987, central bankers around the world were very well aware of this story and had no intention of being cast as the villains as the history of the 1930s repeated itself. In the immediate aftermath of the crash there were prompt and universally applauded efforts to supply the markets with the necessary liquidity, and, even more significantly, short-term nominal interest rates fell by a full percentage point. Mr Greenspan's Fed, in particular, even if it could be blamed for precipitating the crash in the first place, arguably came through this test of its nerve with flying colours. Once the panic struck, it was clear that the Fed was immediately prepared to reverse the monetary stance of the late summer. In the slightly longer term there was also a welcome easing of monetary policy. For the time being inflation fears were mercifully forgotten and the priority was the avoidance of recession. Interest rates did inch upwards again towards the end of 1987, but there was another apparent easing of monetary policy in the New Year. Not until later in 1988 did talk of inflation and the need for higher interest rates begin to resurface once again, and by this time any vigorous monetary policy action was restrained by the imminence of the US presidential election. The prompt action of the monetary authorities, then, in exactly the opposite direction to that of their counterparts in the 1930s, is one of the main reasons why the crash of 1987 passed off relatively easily.

CONCLUSION

In summing up the message of the 1987 stock market crash, the conclusion must be drawn that if it was indeed true that one of the main causes of the crash was the move to higher interest rates and tighter monetary policy in the summer of 1987, the markets decisively rejected that policy. The crisis forced the hand of the monetary authorities to undo that trend and pursue a more relaxed monetary course, at least for the time being. Paradoxically, therefore, the result of the crash, combined with the fact that 1988 was an election year in the USA, was actually to avoid a recession (which otherwise might have been deliberately induced by the monetary authorities) in that year.

As soon as the US election was over, however, inflation became the focus of attention once more, and early 1989 saw a trend back to tight money and high interest rates. This situation did indeed eventually turn into the next disinflationary recession of 1990/91.

As suggested earlier, the strange reaction nowadays of the stock markets to 'good' economic news, often combined with a positive response when the economic indicators are *poor* in a particular week or month, is in itself a rather eloquent commentary on the state of the conventional wisdom on macroeconomic policymaking at the end of the twentieth century.

NOTES

1. *Successful Investing & Money Management*, vol. 9, p. 6, Toronto: Hume Publishing Company Limited, 1986.
2. 'TSE falls as early confidence dissipates', *Financial Post* (Toronto), 1 December 1994.
3. See 'Extraordinary butchery', *The Economist*, 24 October 1987, and 'Panic propelled the pandemonium', *Globe & Mail* (Toronto), 24 October 1987.
4. Note that, unlike in 1987, the 1929 crash actually occurred after a downturn in economic activity had begun a few months earlier.
5. For example, consider the comment of an 'analyst' quoted in the *Globe & Mail* (Toronto), 20 October 1987: 'Confidence today has just about collapsed...I would expect economic activity to slow down abruptly, and soon...[it is]...a very scary phenomenon.'
6. See, for example, 'After the crash: six months later', *Financial Post* (Toronto), 19 April 1988.
7. 'One-armed policymaker: a survey of the world economy', *The Economist*, 24 September 1988.
8. See 'Baker's words', *The Globe & Mail* (Toronto), 20 October 1987.
9. L. Thurow, 'Bank problems worse than market crash', *Financial Post* (Toronto), 26 October 1988.
10. 'The City staggers to the Lawson beat', *The Economist*, 15 August 1987.

9. Concluding remarks

David Smith (1992: 1), in an interesting book on the relatively recent ups and downs of the British economy, *From Boom to Bust*, quotes Keynes's (1936: 322) opinion that:

> The right remedy for the trade cycle is not to be found in abolishing booms and thus keeping us permanently in a state of semi-slump; but in abolishing slumps and keeping us permanently in a quasi boom.

Keynes's prescription is then dismissed by Smith, however, as 'deliberately overstated'. A more generous view, and that taken in this book, is that Keynes meant exactly what he said, even if he ultimately failed to find the right formula to persuade the rest of the economics profession, economic policymakers and financial journalists.

In effect, the preferred macroeconomic policy option since the 'Revenge of the Rentiers' beginning in the late 1970s and early 1980s, has actually been the other alternative implicitly suggested by Keynes. This is the wrong, rather than the right, remedy. Keeping the economy 'permanently in a state of semi-slump', via tight-money policy and high interest rates, would not be an inaccurate description of the course of events in the industrialized economies over the past two decades. From the point of view of society as a whole, however, such a policy is ultimately self-defeating, and could conceivably even threaten the survival of the system itself.

Certain contemporary economic theorists would like to draw our attention away from the awkward issues of unemployment and recurring recessions. The business cycle is regarded either as not very important (which, indeed, it may not seem to be from the point of view of someone whose own position is very secure), or even as positively desirable, an 'optimal' response to economic shocks and uncertainty. In any event, according to this view, economists should not bother about unemployment and recessions and should rather concentrate on a more rarefied study of the forces determining the theoretical long-run economic growth path. Unfortunately for this perspective, the real world issues do have a nasty habit of eventually forcing their way on to the political agenda, as they have done throughout history. Moreover, economists who argue this way ignore the fact that Keynes's policy of eliminating the slumps would, by definition, raise the average rate of growth.

At a more practical level, it is obvious that policies designed to promote full employment, specifically low real interest rates, increased investment, and expansive conditions generally, are precisely the same prescriptions that would increase the long-run average rate of growth. The opposite is also true, with very clear implications for the wisdom of 'zero inflation' policies and the like.

Among the factors contributing to our contemporary economic malaise are:

1. a strong revival of the pessimistic view that the economy is somehow an 'external' force, and that economic problems are not amenable to rational thought and action on the part of those most affected;
2. growing apparent acceptance of the argument that economic policy deci- sions should actually be taken out of the hands of democratically-elected parliaments and their electorate and left in the hands of 'technical experts' such as central bankers;
3. a related apparent reluctance to discuss or acknowledge the awkward distributional and structural issues in the capitalist economy, the difficult question of who gets what?

Clearly, the psychological inhibitions surrounding the first of these issues will have to be dispelled if anything is to be done at all. Yet, it seems obvious that if many economic problems are caused, and even deliberately created, by human action, some of the solutions could be also.

As for the idea of a non-political economic agency, acting in the interests of the public as a whole, this is obviously a chimera. What is really meant by an 'independent' central bank is that central bankers will then be more free to act primarily in the interest of their own particular constituency, which will tend to be that of financial institutions and bondholders. In contrast, an institution which is subject to democratic political control is more likely to deliver the policies which the majority of citizens actually want. And, if they do not, there is always the remedy of the ballot box.

Finally, failing to deal honestly with the crucial questions of political economy may well enhance the reputation of the economics profession for scientific detachment, but the price of this is an inability to come up with solutions which have any chance of success, and, in particular, to suggest reasonable or workable compromises between the competing interest groups.

All of these issues will have to be addressed if our current economic system is to continue to be a viable social structure for the twenty-first century.

Bibliography

Asimakopulos, A. (1988), 'The aggregate supply function and the share economy: some early drafts of the *General Theory*', in O.F. Hamouda and J.N. Smithin (eds), *Keynes and Public Policy After Fifty Years*, vol. 2, *Theories and Method*, Aldershot: Edward Elgar, 70–80.

Bagehot, W. (1873; 1915), *Lombard Street*, London: John Murray.

Ball, L., N.G. Mankiw and D. Romer (1988), 'The new Keynesian economics and the output-inflation trade-off', *Brookings Papers on Economic Activity*, I, 1–65.

Barro, R.J. (1984), *Macroeconomics*, 1st ed., New York: Wiley & Sons.

–––––– (1989a), 'Interest rate targeting', *Journal of Monetary Economics*, 23, 1, 3–30.

–––––– (1989b), 'The Ricardian approach to budget deficits', *Journal of Economic Perspectives*, 3, 2, Spring, 37–54.

–––––– (1990), *Macroeconomics*, 3rd ed., New York: Wiley & Sons.

–––––– (1995), 'Inflation and economic growth', *Bank of England Quarterly Bulletin*, 35, 2, 166–76.

Branson, W.H. (1988), 'Sources of misalignment in the 1980s', in R.C. Marston (ed.), *Misalignment of Exchange Rates: Effects on Trade and Industry*, Chicago: University of Chicago Press, 9–31.

Broadus, J.A. (1995), 'Reflections on monetary policy', *Federal Reserve Bank of Richmond Economic Quarterly*, 81, 2, Spring, 1–11.

Brofenbrenner, M. (ed.) (1969), *Is the Business Cycle Obsolete?*, New York: Wiley & Sons.

Brunner, K. (1968), 'The role of money and monetary policy', *Federal Reserve Bank of St. Louis Review*, 50, July, 8–24.

Cagan, P. (1956), 'The monetary dynamics of hyperinflation', in M. Friedman (ed.), *Studies in the Quantity Theory of Money*, Chicago: University of Chicago Press, 25–117.

–––––– (1989), 'Monetarism', in J. Eatwell, M. Milgate and P. Newman (eds), *The New Palgrave: Money*, London: Macmillan, 195–205.

Coddington, A. (1983), *Keynesian Economics: The Search for First Principles*, London: Allen & Unwin.

Conklin, D.W. and A. Sayeed (1983), 'Overview of the deficit debate', in D.W. Conklin and T.J. Courchene (eds), *Deficits: How Big and How Bad?*, Toronto: Ontario Economic Council, 12–54.

Courchene, T.J. (1982), 'Recent Canadian monetary policy 1975–81: reflections of a monetary gradualist', Queens University Discussion Paper, no. 505.

Davidson, P. (1991), *Controversies in Post Keynesian Economics*, Aldershot: Edward Elgar.

——— (1994), *Post Keynesian Macroeconomic Theory; A Foundation for Successful Economic Policies for the Twenty-First Century*, Aldershot: Edward Elgar.

Delors, J. (1990), 'Economic and monetary union at the start of stage one', *Journal of International Securities Markets*, Autumn, 195–7.

Dow, S.C. (1988), 'What happened to Keynes's economics?', in O.F. Hamouda and J.N. Smithin (eds), *Keynes and Public Policy After Fifty Years*, vol. 1, *Economics and Policy*, Aldershot: Edward Elgar, 101–10.

Djilas, M. (1957), *The New Class: An Analysis of the Communist System*, New York: Praeger.

Eichengreen, B. (1993), 'European monetary unification', *Journal of Economic Literature*, 31, September, 1321–57.

Eisner, R. (1986), *How Real is the Federal Deficit?*, New York: The Free Press.

——— (1989), 'Budget deficits: rhetoric and reality', *Journal of Economic Perspectives*, 3, 2, Spring, 73–93.

Feldstein, M.S. (1979), 'The welfare cost of permanent inflation and optimal short-run economic policy', *Journal of Political Economy*, 87, 749–68.

——— (1992), 'Europe's monetary union: the case against EMU', *The Economist*, 13 June, 19–22.

Frankel, J.A. (1992), 'International capital mobility: a review', *American Economic Review*, 82, 2, May, 197–202.

Friedman, B.M. (1988), 'Lessons on monetary policy from the 1980s', *Journal of Economic Perspectives*, 2, 3, Summer, 51–72.

Friedman, M. (1968), 'The role of monetary policy', *American Economic Review*, 58, March, 1–17.

——— (1974), 'Comments on the critics', in R.J. Gordon (ed.), *Milton Friedman's Monetary Framework: A Debate with his Critics*, Chicago: University of Chicago Press, 132–77.

——— (1983), 'Monetarism in rhetoric and in practice', *Bank of Japan Monetary and Economic Studies*, 1, October, 1–14.

Friedman, M. and R. Friedman (1962), *Capitalism and Freedom*, Chicago: University of Chicago Press.

——— (1980), *Free to Choose*, New York: Harcourt Brace Jovanovich.

Friedman, M. and A.J. Schwartz (1963), *A Monetary History of the United States, 1867–1960*, Princeton: Princeton University Press.

Fukayama, F. (1992), *The End of History and The Last Man*, New York: The Free Press.

Galbraith, J.K. (1954; 1979), *The Great Crash 1929*, New York: Avon Books.
—— (1987), *Economics in Perspective: A Critical History*, Boston: Houghton Mifflin.
—— (1994), *A Journey Through Economic Time: A Firsthand View*, Boston: Houghton Mifflin.
Gammill, J.F. and T.A. Marsh (1988), 'Trading activity and price behaviour in the stock and stock index futures market in October 1987', *Journal of Economic Perspectives*, 2, 3, Summer, 25–44.
Goodfriend, M. (1993), 'Interest rate policy and the inflation scare problem: 1979–1992', *Federal Reserve Bank of Richmond Economic Quarterly*, 79, Winter, 1–24.
Goodhart, C.A.E. (1989), 'The conduct of monetary policy', *Economic Journal*, 99, July, 293–346.
Goodwin, R. (1988), 'My life and times in the shadow of Keynes', in O.F. Hamouda and J.N. Smithin (eds), *Keynes and Public Policy After Fifty Years*, vol. 1, *Economics and Policy*, Aldershot: Edward Elgar, 141–5.
Gorbachev, M.S. (1988), *Perestroika: New Thinking for Our Country and the World*, New York: Harper & Row.
Gray, H.P. (1987), 'International crowding out: concept and policy implications', *Eastern Economic Review*, 13, July–September, 193–203.
Graziani, A. (1990), 'The theory of the monetary circuit', *Economies et Societies*, 7, 6, 7–36.
Greenwald, B. and J. Stein (1988), 'The task force report: the reasoning behind the recommendations', *Journal of Economic Perspectives*, 2, 3, Summer, 3–23.
Greenwald, B. and J. Stiglitz (1988), 'Examining alternative economic theories', *Brookings Papers on Economic Activity*, I, 207–60.
Greider, W. (1987), *Secrets of the Temple: How the Federal Reserve Runs the Country*, New York: Simon & Schuster.
Hamouda, O.F. and J.N. Smithin (eds) (1988), *Keynes and Public Policy After Fifty Years*, vol. I, *Economics and Policy*, Aldershot: Edward Elgar.
Harrod, R.F. (1939), 'An essay in dynamic economic theory', *Economic Journal*, 49, 14–33.
Hayek, F.A. von (1944), *The Road to Serfdom*, Chicago: University of Chicago Press.
—— (1989), *The Fatal Conceit: The Errors of Socialism*, Chicago: University of Chicago Press.
Heller, W.W. (1986), 'Activist government: key to growth', *Challenge*, March–April, 4–10.
Hicks, J.R. (1937), 'Mr Keynes and the classics', *Econometrica*, 5, April, 147–59.

—— (1982), *Money, Interest and Wages: Collected Essays in Economic Theory*, vol. II, Oxford: Basil Blackwell.

—— (1983), *Classics and Moderns: Collected Essays in Economic Theory*, vol. III, Oxford: Basil Blackwell.

—— (1986), 'Managing without money', in *Chung-Hua Series of Lectures by Invited Eminent Economists*, Tapei: Academia Sinica.

H.M. Treasury (1929), *Memorandum on Certain Proposals Relating to Unemployment*, Cmnd. 3331, London: HMSO.

Hodgson, G.M. (1988), *Economics and Institutions: A Manifesto for a Modern Institutional Economics*, London: Polity Press.

Hoover, K.D. (1984), 'Two types of monetarism', *Journal of Economic Literature*, 22, March, 58–76.

Humphrey, T.M. (1993), *Money, Banking and Inflation: Essays in the History of Monetary Thought*, Aldershot: Edward Elgar.

Jarrett, J.P. and J.G. Selody (1982), 'The productivity-inflation nexus in Canada, 1963–1979', *Review of Economics and Statistics*, 64, August, 361–7.

Johnson, C. (ed.) (1989), *The Market on Trial*, Lloyds Bank Annual Review, London: Pinter Publishers.

Judd, J.P. and B. Trehan (1995), 'Has the Fed gotten tougher on inflation?', *FRBSF Weekly Letter*, 95–13, March.

Kaldor, N. (1986), *The Scourge of Monetarism*, 2nd ed., Oxford: Oxford University Press.

Kenen, P. (1992), *EMU After Maastricht*, Washington, DC: Group of Thirty.

Keynes, J.M. (1920), *The Economic Consequences of the Peace*, New York: Harcourt Brace Howe.

—— (1923; 1971), *The Collected Writings of John Maynard Keynes*, vol. 4, *A Tract on Monetary Reform*, London: Macmillan for the Royal Economic Society.

—— (1925), *The Economic Consequences of Mr. Churchill*, London: Hogarth Press.

—— (1936), *The General Theory of Employment Interest and Money*, London: Macmillan.

—— (1939), 'Professor Tinbergen's method', *Economic Journal*, 49, 558–68.

—— (1980a), *The Collected Writings of John Maynard Keynes*, vol. 26, *Activities 1940–46: Shaping the Post-War World: Bretton Woods and Reparations*, edited by D. Moggridge, London: Macmillan for the Royal Economic Society.

—— (1980b), *The Collected Writings of John Maynard Keynes*, vol. 27, *Activities 1940–46: Shaping the Post-War World: Employment and Com-*

modities, edited by D. Moggridge, London: Macmillan for the Royal Economic Society.

King, R.G. and C.I. Plosser (1984), 'Money, credit and prices in a real business cycle', *American Economic Review*, 74, 3, 363–80.

Kregel, J. (1985), 'Budget deficits, stabilization policy and liquidity preference: Keynes's postwar policy proposals', in F. Vicarelli (ed.), *Keynes's Revelance Today*, London: Macmillan, 28–50.

Krieger, L. (1969), 'National Socialism or Nazism', in *Encyclopedia International*, vol. 12, New York: Grolier, 452–5.

Kydland, F.E. and E.C. Prescott (1982), 'Time to build and aggregate fluctuations', *Econometrica*, 50, 6, 1345–69.

Laidler, D.E.W. (1990), *Taking Money Seriously and Other Essays*, London: Phillip Allan.

Laudan, L. (1977), *Progress and its Problems: Towards a Theory of Scientific Growth*, London: Routledge & Kegan Paul.

Lavoie, M. (1992a), *Foundations of Post-Keynesian Economic Analysis*, Aldershot: Edward Elgar.

—— (1992b), 'Jacques Le Bourva's theory of endogenous credit money', *Review of Political Economy*, 4, 4, 436–46.

Le Bourva, J. (1992), 'Money creation and credit multipliers', *Review of Political Economy*, 4, 4, 447–66.

Leland H. and M. Rubenstein (1988), 'Comments on the market crash: six months later', *Journal of Economic Perspectives*, 2, 3, Summer, 45–50.

Lipsey, R.G. (ed.) (1990), *Zero Inflation: The Goal of Price Stability*, Toronto: C.D. Howe Institute.

Lucas, R.E. Jr (1981), *Studies in Business-Cycle Theory*, Cambridge, MA: MIT Press.

—— (1987), *Models of Business Cycles*, Oxford: Basil Blackwell.

—— (1988), 'On the mechanics of economic development', *Journal of Monetary Economics*, 22, 1, July, 3–42.

Lucas, R.E. Jr and T.J. Sargent (1981), 'After Keynesian macroeconomics', in R.E. Lucas Jr. and T.J. Sargent (eds), *Rational Expectations and Econometric Practice*, London: Allen & Unwin, 295–320.

McCallum, B.T. (1986), 'On "real" and "sticky-price" theories of the business cycle', *Journal of Money, Credit, and Banking*, 18, 4, 397–414.

—— (1989), *Monetary Economics: Theory and Policy*, New York: Macmillan.

—— (1995), 'Rules for monetary policy', *NBER Reporter*, Spring, 5–7.

McLean, B. and L. Osberg (eds) (forthcoming), *The Unemployment Crisis: All for Nought?*, Montreal & Kingston: Queens University Press.

McQuaig, L. (1995), *Shooting the Hippo: Death by Deficit and Other Canadian Myths*, Toronto: Viking.

Mankiw, N.G. (1992), *Macroeconomics*, 1st ed., New York: Worth Publishers.

Marston, R.C. (1988), 'Exchange rate policy reconsidered', *Economic Impact*, 62, 11–15.

Marx, K. (1859; 1970), *A Contribution to the Critique of Political Economy*, Moscow: Progress Publishers.

Matthews, R.C.O. (1968), 'Why has Britain had full employment since the War?', *Economic Journal*, 78, September, 555–69.

Meltzer, A.H. (1988), *Keynes's Monetary Theory: A Different Interpretation*, Cambridge: Cambridge University Press.

Mirowski, P. (1989), *More Heat than Light: Economics as Social Physics: Physics as Nature's Economics*, Cambridge: Cambridge University Press.

Mises, L. von (1978), *Notes and Recollections*, South Holland, Illinois: Libertarian Press.

Modigliani, F. (1944), 'Liquidity preference and the theory of interest and money', *Econometrica*, 12, January, 45–88.

——— (1983), 'Government deficits, inflation and future generations', in D.W. Conklin and T.J. Courchene (eds), *Deficits: How Big and How Bad?*, Toronto: Ontario Economic Council, 12–54.

Moore, B.M. (1988), *Horizontalists and Verticalists: The Macroeconomics of Credit Money*, Cambridge: Cambridge University Press.

Mundell, R. (1963), 'Inflation and real interest', *Journal of Political Economy*, 71, 280–3.

Nerlove, M. (1958), 'Adaptive expectations and cobweb phenomena', *Quarterly Journal of Economics*, 72, 227–40.

Paglia, C. (1994), *Vamps and Tramps: Further Essays*, New York: Vintage Books.

Palley, T.I. (forthcoming), 'The institutionalization of deflationary monetary policy', in A.J. Cohen, H. Hagemann, and J.N. Smithin (eds), *Money, Financial Institutions and Macroeconomics*, Boston: Kluwer Academic Publishers.

Paraskevopoulos, C.C., Paschakis, J. and J.N. Smithin (forthcoming), 'Is monetary sovereignty an option for the small open economy?', *North American Journal of Economics and Finance*.

Parguez, A. (1993a), 'Budget austerity in France', English translation of a paper published in P. Paquette and M. Seccareccia (eds), *Les Pieges de l'Austerite: Dette Nationale et Prosperitie Economique: Alternative a l'Orthodoxie*, Montreal: PUM.

——— (1993b), 'Beyond scarcity: a reappraisal of the theory of the monetary circuit', mimeo, Paris: ISMEA.

Parkin, M. (1982), *Modern Macroeconomics*, 1st ed., Scarborough, Ont.: Prentice-Hall Canada.

———— (1994), 'The rise and fall of inflation', mimeo, University of Western Ontario, October, 28pp.

Pheby, J.D. (1988), *Methodology and Economics: A Critical Introduction*, London: Macmillan.

Phillips, A.W. (1958), 'The relation between unemployment and the rate of change of money wages in the United Kingdom, 1861–1957', *Economica*, 25, November, 283–99.

Pressman, S. (1987), 'The policy relevance of the *General Theory*', *Journal of Economic Studies*, 14, 4, 13–23.

Rebelo, S. (1991), 'Long run policy analysis and long run growth', *Journal of Political Economy*, 99, 3, June, 500–21.

Ricardo, D. (1817; 1973), *The Principles of Political Economy and Taxation*, edited by D. Winch, London: J.M. Dent & Sons.

Robertson, D. (1934), 'Industrial fluctuations and the natural rate of interest', *Economic Journal*, 44, 650–6.

Robinson, J. (1964), *Economic Philosophy*, Harmondsworth: Pelican Books.

Rogers, C. (1989), *Money, Interest and Capital: A Study in the Foundations of Monetary Theory*, Cambridge: Cambridge University Press.

Romer, C.D. (1986a), 'Spurious volatility in historical unemployment data', *Journal of Political Economy*, 94, February, 1–37.

———— (1986b), 'Is the stabilization of the postwar economy a figment of the data?', *American Economic Review*, 76, 3, June, 314–34.

Romer, C.D. and D.H. Romer (1995), 'An overview of monetary policy', *NBER Reporter*, Spring, 8–11.

Romer, P.M. (1986), 'Increasing Returns and Long-Run Growth', *Journal of Political Economy*, 94, 5, October, 1002–37.

Samuelson, P.A. (1947; 1983), *Foundations of Economic Analysis: Enlarged Edition*, Cambridge, MA: Harvard University Press.

———— (1983), 'Introduction', in *Foundations of Economic Analysis: Enlarged Edition*, Cambridge, MA: Harvard University Press, xv–xxvi.

Sargent, T.J. and N. Wallace (1975), 'Rational expectations, the optimal monetary instrument and the optimum money supply rule', *Journal of Political Economy*, 83, April, 241–54.

———— (1981), 'Some unpleasant monetarist arithmetic', *Federal Reserve Bank of Minneapolis Quarterly Review*, 5, 1–17.

Schumpeter, J.A. (1942; 1975), *Capitalism, Socialism and Democracy*, New York: Harper & Row.

Seccareccia, M. (1993), 'Keynesianism and public investment: re-evaluating social-democratic goals within a left-Keynesian perspective', working paper no. 9307E, Department of Economics, University of Ottawa.

Sekine, T.T. (1993), 'Fordism, casino capital and the current Japanese recession', paper presented to JSAC/93 in Montreal, October, 30pp.

Selgin, G.A. (1990), 'The price level, productivity and macroeconomic order', mimeo, University of Georgia, October, 101pp.

Selgin, G.A. and L.H. White (1994), 'How would the invisible hand handle money?', *Journal of Economic Literature*, 32, December, 1718–49.

Sennholz, H.F. (1978), 'Postscript', in L. von Mises, *Notes and Recollections*, South Holland, Illinois: Libertarian Press, 145–76.

Skidelsky, R. (1992), *John Maynard Keynes: The Economist as Saviour 1920–37*, London: Macmillan.

Smith, A. (1776; 1970), *An Inquiry into the Nature and Causes of the Wealth of Nations*, Harmondsworth: Pelican Books.

Smith, D. (1992), *From Boom to Bust: Trial and Error in British Economic Policy*, Harmondsworth: Penguin Books.

Smithin, J.N. (1982), 'Two "contradictions" in the economic and social development of the Soviet bloc', *Kosmas: Journal of Czechoslovak and Central European Studies*, 1, 2, Winter, 51–62.

―――― (1985), 'The market mechanism versus the historical process as the source of economic controversy', *Economic Notes*, 14, 1, 169–76.

―――― (1989), 'The composition of government expenditures and the effectiveness of fiscal policy', in J.D. Pheby (ed.), *New Directions in Post Keynesian Economics*, Aldershot: Edward Elgar, 192–207.

―――― (1990), *Macroeconomics After Thatcher and Reagan: The Conservative Policy Revolution in Retrospect*, Aldershot: Edward Elgar.

―――― (1991), 'European monetary arrangements and national economic sovereignty', in A. Amin and M. Dietrich (eds), *Towards a New Europe?: Structural Change in the European Economy*, Aldershot: Edward Elgar, 191–211.

―――― (1994a), *Controversies in Monetary Economics: Ideas, Issues and Policy*, Aldershot: Edward Elgar.

―――― (1994b), 'Cause and effect in the relationship between budget deficits and the rate of interest', *Economies et Societies*, 28, 1–2, January–February, 151–69.

―――― (1995a), 'Geldpolitik und Demokratie', in C. Thomasberger (ed.), *Europaische Geldpolitik zwischen Marktzwangen und neuen institutionellen Regelungun: Zur politischen Okonomie der europaischen Wahrungintegration*, Marburg: Metropolis-Verlag, 73–96.

―――― (1995b), 'Econometrics and the "facts of experience"', in I. Rima (ed.), *Measurement, Quantification, and Economic Analysis*, London: Routledge, 363–78.

―――― (forthcoming), 'Real interest rates and unemployment', in B. McLean and L. Osberg (eds), *The Unemployment Crisis: All for Nought?*, Montreal & Kingston: Queen's University Press.

Smithin, J.N. and B.M. Wolf (1993), 'What would be a "Keynesian" approach to currency and exchange rate issues?', *Review of Political Economy*, 5, 3, July, 365–83.

Snowden, B., H. Vane and P. Wynarczyk (1994), *A Modern Guide to Macroeconomics: An Introduction to Competing Schools of Thought*, Aldershot: Edward Elgar.

Solow, R.M. (1956), 'A contribution to the theory of economic growth', *Quarterly Journal of Economics*, 70, 65–94.

——— (1986), 'Unemployment: getting the questions right', *Economica*, 53 (supplement), S23–34.

Stanford, J. (1995), 'The impact of real competitiveness on monetary policy and exchange rates in an open economy', in paper presented at a conference on Money, Financial Institutions and Macroeconomics, York University, Toronto, April.

Stein, H. (1989), *Governing the $5 Trillion Economy*, New York: Oxford University Press.

Stock, J.H. and M. Watson (1988), 'Variable trends in economic time series', *Journal of Economic Perspectives*, 2, 3, Summer, 147–74.

Summers, L.H. (1991), 'The scientific illusion in empirical macroeconomics', *Scandanavian Journal of Economics*, 93, 129–48.

Taylor, J.B. (1993), 'Discretion versus policy rules in practice', *Carnegie-Rochester Conference Series on Public Policy*, 39, 195–214.

Temin P. (1989), *Lessons from the Great Depression*, Cambridge, Mass: MIT Press.

Thornton, H. (1802; 1962), *An Inquiry into the Nature and Effects of the Paper Credit of Great Britain*, edited by F.A. von Hayek, New York: Augustus M. Kelley.

Tobin, J. (1985), 'Monetarism: an ebbing tide?', *The Economist*, 27 April, 23–5.

——— (1986a), 'High time to restore the Employment Act of 1946', *Challenge*, May–June, 4–12.

——— (1986b), 'The future of Keynesian Economics', *Eastern Economic Journal*, 12, 4, October–December, 347–56.

——— (1993), 'Thinking straight about fiscal stimulus and deficit reduction', *Challenge*, March–April, 15–18.

Wicksell, K. (1898; 1965), *Interest and Prices*, translated by R.F. Kahn, New York: Augustus M. Kelley.

Wray, L.R. (1992), 'Alternative approaches to money and interest rates', *Journal of Economic Issues*, 26, 4, 1–33.

Yellen, J.L. (1989), 'Symposium on the budget deficit', *Journal of Economic Perspectives*, 3, 2, Spring, 17–21.

NEWSPAPERS AND PERIODICALS CONSULTED

Bank of Canada Review (Ottawa)
Economic & Social Action (Toronto)
The Economist (London)
The Globe & Mail (Toronto)
The Financial Post (Toronto)
World Economic Outlook (IMF, Washington DC)

Index